WHEN THE FANS GO HOME
THE DREAM WEEK THAT NEVER ENDED

J.P. QUINN

When the Fans Go Home

Copyright © 2023 by J.P. Quinn

All rights reserved.

Published by Red Penguin Books

Bellerose Village, New York

ISBN

Print 978-1-63777-434-2, 978-1-63777-435-9

Digital 978-1-63777-433-5

No part of this book may be reproduced in any form or by any electronic or mechanical means, including information storage and retrieval systems, without written permission from the author, except for the use of brief quotations in a book review.

*This book is dedicated to my good friend, Patrick,
the 2019 Devo's Desperados,
all the players and pros who helped make the experience
unforgettable,
my brother-in-law, Danny, who planted the seed with endless tales
of his prior experience of Dream Week,
and Tara, who without her selflessness and support this experience
and book would have never been realized and conceived.*

CONTENTS

Foreword	vii
Introduction	ix

PART ONE
THE ESSENCE OF COMPETITION

The Birth of Competition	3
Preparing for Greatness	23

PART TWO
THE EXPERIENCE BEGINS

The Arrival	43
Excellence Beyond Winning	61
The Banquet and Goodbyes	91

PART THREE
TAKING ACTION

Goal Setting	97
Mentoring/Coaching For Successful Performance:	107
Learn How to Deal With Losing	109
Epilogue	113
Acknowledgments	115
About the Author	117

FOREWORD

As with any meaningful adventure or undertaking, there must be a purpose and a plan as well as a source of motivation. This book discusses from where purpose comes, how the plan is developed, and the motivation that turned one goal into a healthy obsession and way of life. Everything I did for more than six months was directed at getting to Orioles Dream Week healthy and ready to perform at my absolute best. It is only in reflection after the fact that I can fully engage in thoughtfulness about my motivation and drive to achieve that goal. I will delve into detail about goal setting and maintaining motivation. I will also discuss the pitfalls that arose throughout the process as I prepared my mind and body for this competition.

In the second half of the book, I discuss the desire I had to attend Dream Week and be competitive. As I delve deeper, there are three main objectives to identify which are: what type of motivation was I using, how well did I do with obstacles, and did I give equal attention to preparing my mind and body? There is always a balance between the "have to" and "get to" in life. The approach I took, as well as what I learned during this undertaking, are also addressed. The investment of money and time were significant and provided fuel to the fire of motivation.

FOREWORD

While those motivators burn hot, they also burn out fast. As we journey together, I hope you will see the longer, slow-burning fuel that sustained me over the months leading up to Dream Week.

Let's get started!

INTRODUCTION

Thank you for buying or gifting this book forward. To the reader, I hope you find this book entertaining as well as impactful for your own life whether or not you have ever attended a Dream Week event. It is not even critical that you have a love and passion for baseball or that you have studied in the field of Sports Psychology as have I. What is important is that you have a desire to be connected to people and events. More than a book about baseball and living a dream, it is a story of hope and optimism and learning to integrate them as a part of my daily routine. Baseball and life are similar in that you can choose to be a spectator or a participant; but if you want to participate, like baseball, life is a skill. You either feed the passion or it will fade away. That is the distinction between surviving and thriving. What I have learned on this journey is that where I once saw obstacles, I now see opportunities, and where I once defined failure, I now define growth. There is great peace of mind in finding who you are when you ignore what the world wants you to be. This book is not intended to simply make you feel better today but rather to spark a desire to be better than yesterday with a vision of greatness for tomorrow.

INTRODUCTION

What great fortune it is to have the wisdom of an old man, the spirit of a child and the energy of a teenager, at least for one week of eternity.

- J.P. Quinn

PART ONE
THE ESSENCE OF COMPETITION

THE BIRTH OF COMPETITION

It is an interesting concept that competition is born from something. In all actuality, it is taught to us. As we learn about feelings of success and failure, we develop a sense of what we want to achieve in competition and in life, as well. We mature into a set of values that determines how we compete. Do we cheat in order to win at any cost, or do we see value in fair play? All this grows and becomes more defined from the birth of competition. Do I take a performance-enhancing drug, use a video device to steal pitches, or cork my bat? What is it we truly hope to gain from competition? Of course, the fuel that drives our competition engine is in the goal from which it originates.

In developing a goal, there are several planning phases that must occur before action is taken. If action does occur without a planning phase, it typically does not last and has little direction. It will become disorganized. Like a child running down a hill, it usually ends up in an ataxia of soup sandwich. So, even before Dream Week became a goal, it was merely a concept, an idea born from the never-ending stories told by my brother-in-law, Danny. He had attended Orioles Dream Week two years earlier and, by all accounts, had surpassed every amazing Facebook post and adventure I had done previously. I was once the envy of all my friends, having attended every major sporting event known to man and had even played in the World Series of Poker; but with one grand week in Sarasota, Danny took the title of cool experiences. Now, there was no way I was going to live with that. I had to find a way to experience Dream Week myself!

FAMILY COMPETITION

I think everyone has some level of competition in their family, but to understand the level I grew up with and adapted to with my sister and brother-in-law, I feel it necessary to give you some background. Early on, I associated competition more with self-survival than most think of in sports or other events. When I was in eighth grade, on the day of my Confirmation, my sister, Kelly, chased me around the house with a knife. The reason was that if I could keep her from killing me and make it to Confirmation, I may have a possibility of going to heaven. She argued that she would kill me before Confirmation, thus sending me to no better status than purgatory and most likely hell for not fulfilling my Catholic obligation. As she chased after me with the knife, I ran out the back door, around to the front door, back inside, and locked her out of the home.

She pounded on the screen door in an unheralded rage like something you'd see in a horror film. The screen door, which still had the winter glass in place of the screen, eventually succumbed to her relentless pounding, and she broke the glass, cutting her hand open in the process. She then ditched the knife over the backyard fence. When my parents returned home and saw her hand bleeding, I immediately recounted the events as they happened, but without evidence of the knife, my story was too fantastic to believe. My sister, of course, concocted a story in which she was simply taking out the trash when I locked her out without cause, and she cut her hand on the glass while knocking on the door to get back in. My mother slapped me for lying on the day I was going to be confirmed.

Some 20 years later as we sat around the crab table at my parents' home in Ocean Pines, Maryland, thankfully and for some inexplicable reason, Kelly finally confessed to the true events of that day and many others of which I had initially been blamed in the past. The second half of my life since has been lived with unrepentant retribution for the torture I endured as a child at the hands of my older sister. I am sure younger siblings all over the world are living vicariously through the hope of redemption I have given them in this moment. Though the victim mentality does not suit me well, I have taken full advantage of the catering that my mother has given me in the years since.

While my intent is not to garner some favor toward me and resentment toward my sister, though it would be an appealing natural consequence, it illustrates the sheer intensity of our rivalry and how far we have each gone to one up the other. The Irish are known for their ability to embellish facts and create dramatic effect. To no surprise, our family embraced these stereotypes, among others, and adopted such characteristics. That being said, it is with the utmost sincerity that I remain factual in my accounts of all subsequent and following events, but it may be inherent that "truth" and "facts" be redefined to appropriately match the emotion of the moment. Of course, had the only family rivalry involved my sister and myself, it would be less than impactful to this story. So now, I must introduce into the mix my brother-in-law, Danny.

It is difficult to describe Danny because many people who meet him do not understand or get him. Imagine the strength and loyalty of a German Shepherd with the intensity of the Looney Toons' Tasmanian Devil. He has great conviction and unwavering beliefs but not always a clear sense of social awareness. Well, to say he is not socially aware may be unfair. I think he is often aware but just not empathetic to counter viewpoints. Like a German Shepherd, he will welcome you in but is close to attacking if you do not assimilate to his environment. He has a keen sense of what is right and wrong, and if it aligns with your belief system, then you find yourself in an engaging conversation. However, if your beliefs, opinions, or values differ from an acceptable deviation, expect to be challenged, asked rhetorical questions that you will not have time to answer before he provides the correct one for you, and feeling inept for even having an opinion on the matter.

One of my favorite stories to tell about Danny is the one where we were all playing the Seinfeld trivia game at my parents' home during one Christmas gathering. It was believed that this would be a safe alternative to the former game we played, Monopoly. On occasion, we still find small green houses under furniture and Community Cards behind appliances from the last time we played many years ago, though the Boardwalk property card hasn't been seen since. Anyway, as the years have progressed, the few rules that exist in the Seinfeld game have been enforced vigorously and without exception. Despite these stringent applications of the vague rules, I have dominated every year we have played, and I intended that this year would be no exception. To set the stage, the participants this year were myself (the defending champion), my brother-in-law (the disgruntled contender), my sister (the antagonist, aka pot stirrer), and my then-wife, Tara (the rookie).

I had prepared my wife for the level of competition and seriousness that things happen in my family, and my description of the upcoming events prompted her to buy the card game and to try and memorize as many trivial facts about the show as possible. This is the first time that secret has been exposed, and by doing so, I may be risking forfeiture of the 2017 Christmas results. In the first round, I was not allowed a partial answer by my brother-in-law, making the competition closer than I was comfortable with, but I eventually prevailed. It was in the second game, however, that things took a turn toward catastrophe. My brother-in-law, who was gaining momentum and ground on me, gave a partially incorrect answer, much like the

Seinfeld episode of "Moops" itself; and when I took the point away, the Tasmanian Devil side of my brother-in-law came out. Between dodging the epitaphs laced in spit, the playing board and all its pieces became victim to the tornadic episode that ensued! The event was further fueled by my sister who, in the resulting hysteria, calmly uttered, "So who won?" Kelly has an uncanny ability, almost instinctual, to find that open wound and figuratively pouring salt in it. Actually, if it amused her, I believe she would have occasion to literally pour salt into an open wound. We haven't spoken about that game since, and writing about it here may reignite a dormant fuse but a necessary risk to capture the level of intense competition within our family.

The most interesting thing about our family dynamic is that anyone integrated into the family becomes conditioned to this level of intense competition. Before she became my wife, Tara once stated "I don't care who wins as long as we have fun." I immediately and unintentionally took that as a challenge and gradually, over time, created this beautiful monster who became as vicious a competitor as anyone. So much so that the night before our wedding in Ocean City, while walking the boardwalk hand in hand, we came across the horse race game where you roll balls into designated numbered holes and advance your horse to the finish line.

I had bragged for decades that since the age of 12 I had never been defeated. She looked at me and asked if I wanted to go against her to which I emphatically declined, stating that I was a retired champion. At this time, she took a brilliant tactic of subtleness, not typical for my family, and responded with a simple under the breath "Hmph." The artistic passive-aggressive tactic worked, and I hastily accepted the challenge, not taking in the potential consequences of my actions. During the race, my balls clinked when they should have clanged, swerved when they should have swayed, dipped when they should have dumped, and suddenly it was over. She beat me decisively.

With pride on her face and disgust on mine, we went back

up the boardwalk from where we came, this time not hand in hand as she clutched her winning stuffed pony as if it were the Stanley Cup. The happiness of her victory, however, was short lived with my intentional response, "Thank you for stealing my one childhood memory that had previously provided all my confidence to succeed." The smile disappeared from her face, and my competitive heart was once again restored. While all was eventually forgiven and we had many moments of marital bliss after, the activities of that night did set a precedent for future conversations I had not foreseen in the moment.

THE VALUE OF COMPETITION

One of the things I have learned throughout my life and now especially working in the field of sports and performance psychology is that competition can be productive, improve self-efficacy, and build social bonds especially with people who matter to you in your life. The unfortunate reality, however, is that we are often coached at an early age to "destroy our enemy" and that winning above all is what matters. This mindset is a shift to our natural tendency to compete. If you think I am being obtuse to the nature of competition, tell two little children to play a game together. Instinctively, they will help each other out with implementing rules, fair play, and even cooperation of strategy. It is only through our experience that we learn to value winning over learning. Just ask the 2017 Houston Astros!

I remember this theory explicitly when I played college baseball. I pitched in a fall game against a JUCO. That stands for Junior College in case you are not fully aware of the acronyms of collegiate sports. I was attending a four-year college and felt that there was no way a junior college should be playing on the same field as us even though I, myself, was only a freshman. Most athletes agree that fall baseball is much like spring football in that the main attention is paid to learning, adjusting, and trying out newly-acquired skills and plays. Of course, with my upbringing that winning is everything, I was only focused on the outcome, not skill acquisition. While we won the game, I did hang a curveball that was hit out of the park. This was unacceptable to me at the time. Even though I got the outcome I so desperately wanted, since a mistake occurred during my performance, I refused to shake hands with the opposing players. This was because, to me, it was not a good game at all, and I was not going to dare be ceremonial and participate in such lies. Even with the win, I took whatever enjoyment I may have had and sabotaged it under the disguise of disgust. And yes, I know what you are probably thinking of me, and you can say it because I was being an ass. The worst part is, I don't even think I was actually disappointed in my performance, but I think I was expected to be disappointed whenever a mistake was made.

When children learn at an early age, before cognitive processes are fully developed, that the person on the other side of the field is the opponent and any evaluation of success is measured by how well you beat that opponent, it is no wonder why we develop a sense of disdain for other teams even as we become fans in adult life. What happens if you put two seemingly civilized people in the same room and during the conversation, one identifies as a Washington Whatever fan and the other a Dallas Cowboy fan? A Baltimore Ravens fan and a Pittsburg Steelers fan? Or an Alabama Tide fan and the rest of the country? The point is well understood that how one fan sees another in the context of the person they are, their level of intelligence, and even their physical attractiveness can be based on their allegiance to their team. As ridiculous as it seems to be, somehow it becomes reasonable in the moment.

What may be even more absurd is that we base the quality of a person to be higher if they are also a fan of the same team. I have not been contacted by Stanford yet to conduct this study, but I have reasonable knowledge from prior studies. I've read, and it is widely known, that you will find people more attractive, and even more trustworthy if they have allegiance to or are in the same fan base as yourself! If I meet an Orioles fan who remembers where they were when Scott McGregor got the final out in game five of the 1983 World Series and can name the entire roster, I may give them the key to my house. Some may argue that the same thing is seen based on political or religious beliefs, but these systems are different in that they are deeply-held beliefs and values we hold as human beings. The jersey or hat a person wears is not as deeply rooted but does pull upon those deeply-held values. Since most of these values are instilled in us at an early age and become foundational, they do not usually change over time. It makes sense then that the values we teach children about competition early on are what they will carry with them throughout their lives, and I was not immune to this mentality.

One thing I did have was that I have been fortunate to acquire an advanced education, though my life experience sometimes clashes and conflicts with those teachings. The interesting thing I found about higher education is that sometimes you learn things about yourself that you did not know and even more so are reluctant to accept. I hope as we journey together through this story you will discover that the beliefs and values I had around competition may not be all that dissimilar from many of yours, the most common being that winning is valued above all things. This misunderstood value has cheated me during many of my competitions, in and out of sports. If you are reading this now and thinking well, yes, winning is the only thing that matters and defines the measure of success, then stay with me. In time, I will reveal how you can always win, but for now I will focus on how I perceived competition and what values I placed upon it.

Thinking back, a long way back, I remember the first time I played on a team and the coach telling us that we win as a team and we lose as a team. I soon realized that wasn't really the truth. We all knew who the superstar players were and who the jacked-up players were. If someone dropped a ball in the outfield (like me) and the opposing winning run scored as a result, the non-verbal communication let me know it was my fault despite our unified cheer of, "2-4-6-8 who do we appreciate…" which, by the way was always one of my most despised cheers. It was inescapably obvious as a pre-adolescent child who the strong players were because they had that extra oomph of testosterone that was delayed in the majority of others; and yet, even as I began to catch up to the rest of the pack, the mindset of bad and talented players was at the forefront of my thinking especially as my talent finally started tipping the scale toward the "strong player" side. Even into emerging adulthood as a college athlete as I described earlier, there were times after a game I would not line up and say the customary "good game" to the opposing team because maybe in my mind it was not a good game. And sometimes it was not just due to my own performance. I was quick to assign blame to others, as well. Sometimes our players really sucked, or maybe the umpire was squeezing the strike zone on me, forcing me to throw gift pitches in the zone. Any number of things may have caused me to feel like it was not a good game, and more times than not it was things that were largely out of my control.

So, what I learned from my early experiences about competition is that it was all about the outcome, the win or loss. This resulted in a subversive desire for players on my team to be the ones to make a mistake or give up a home run so that it would not be my fault if we lost or, even better, I could come in and save the game from an otherwise inevitable disaster. I was extremely focused on my own individual performance and accomplishments and took immense pride in them. The sole measure of my performance was based entirely on the outcome. This bled over into every other activity I did, including games such as Monopoly or even bowling at a birthday party. Whatever it was, I did not want to lose; and if I did, I immediately looked at the conditions that caused it. This was the way I defined my resiliency and adaptability. To this day, I still have challenges finding the purpose in any outcome other than winning.

EDUCATION AND EXPERIENCE

As I aged and found that I was no longer young or physically fit enough to do law enforcement and had pretty much burned out on social work after about ten years of counseling people who had no desire to help themselves and constantly made excuses while swearing to God they were going to change, I decided to go back to school and get my master's degree in Sport and Performance Psychology. I briefly ran a baseball academy when I lived in Arizona and really enjoyed teaching young athletes how to improve their fundamental skills and mental fortitude to perform at their best. I figured that advancing my education would be the best way to advance a career in coaching and instructing baseball players and other athletes.

There are inevitable crossroads in life, sometimes several; and at these crossroads, we find where our experience, passion, desire, and energy converge to steer us in a direction that best suits our desires to feel autonomous and purposeful. Being purposeful is often overlooked and yet is one of the most critical factors in maintaining motivation in life and the things we take pride in accomplishing. To unpack this concept even more, our core values are what drive us and make us feel proud and purposeful in what we do. Think about those things that hold most true to you, the core of who you are and those are your values. The challenge of fulfilling a life mission to our values is that our beliefs get in the way. For example, I value honesty because, for me, it is the cornerstone of building trust and confidence in those I work or socialize with. Sometimes, I do not always follow that value because my belief is that people tend to lie, especially if they feel uncomfortable or threatened in some way. I also believe that sometimes people lie just to take advantage or get what they want in that moment, either tangible or not. My beliefs about other people impact my behaviors and threaten my value system. This conflict can become enraging and disrupt motivation to do the things that make me feel purposeful. It also impacts my autonomy because when I allow beliefs to overshadow values, I am now acting on someone else and not myself.

So, at my crossroads, I decided that going back to school made sense and doing something related to sport and performance fit into those categories of experience, passion, desire, and energy, so I enrolled at the University of the Rockies. Since it had been a minute (24 years to be exact) that I had gone to undergraduate school, I didn't have a valid GRE or Graduate Readiness Exam score that would allow me entry into most programs. I went in under a probationary status that was lifted after completion of my first three classes, each of which I received an A. One of the interesting things that happened early in the program is that my previous ideals of competition were tremendously challenged, and by the halfway point, I came to realize that I did not understand anything about competition based on how I was brought up in sports. In fact, I had to reprogram my brain to differentiate between competition, performance, and results because up to now they were one and the same.

If you recall a little while ago, I said that if winning is the most important thing to you, then stand by and I would reveal the secret that was given to me, my light bulb moment in understanding the difference between the three. So here it is: if you want a guarantee to win, play far below your competition. That's it! It is almost as much of a guarantee as you will get in life, but not as mind-blowing as you probably anticipated. So why not? Sure, as a high school athlete or a collegiate pitcher I could go to a little league baseball game and probably pitch a perfect game, strike out the side of every inning, so why is that not satisfying if winning is all that matters? Of course, it is because the competition is not at the level of the opposing player or team. In fact, it should be quite embarrassing to see such a spectacle. It can be assumed then that winning in and of itself is not the most important thing.

I remember playing basketball in the 10-12 age bracket, and we had a kid on our team that was well over six foot tall. All we had to do was pass the ball to him and he could shoot or dunk over anyone. Every game that was the plan. Pass the ball to George and he would score. We went on to win the championship that year and I got myself a nice big trophy. This was an era before everyone got trophies, so it was kind of a big deal to go to the banquet and get an award. The funny thing about it, though, is I remember going home and throwing the trophy away. I was so angry about getting the trophy because I knew that I didn't score more than one basket the entire season; no one did, except George. Even at an early age, I knew there was something more to competition than just winning.

Looking back, I think there was something inside me that accepted defeat as long as I knew I was playing against the best and they were giving it their all. As a child, I had a best friend, Chris Cain. We met when we were three and remained best friends up until high school. Chris was a combination of Robert Redford, John Travolta, and James Dean. Yeah, he was that cool! He had the looks and the talent that few are blessed with at an early age. As for myself, I was described by my cautious yet eternally optimistic mother as a "late bloomer." My dad was more colorful in his description of me. He would say I was "like a puppy dog, what I didn't eat or piss on I'd just chew up or tear up." In early adulthood terms, I was what you might call a good wingman. Chris and I played every sport together and he pretty much beat me at everything, even games that we made up. It was never that close. We had fun, though, and over time the scores did become more competitive, and I was able to close the gap the more I tried. This lesson was important when it came to developing my resilience later in life because I learned that even in defeat, I can still learn and become better the next time I compete.

I do feel that those who knew me as a young child and emerging adult would say I have given myself too much credit in the aforementioned paragraph because in many of those early moments I was not a gracious loser or humble winner. It took me a long time to develop an understanding of competition and why I have made it not only the introduction to this book, but also a point of emphasis. Competition in sport or any performance is productive and energizing when viewed through the appropriate lens. Perhaps it is in the definition of performance itself that we often fail to understand and make everything, even things that do not matter a competition and that is when it can become destructive.

Performances in the world of sport and performance psychology have specific criteria that need to be met to constitute a performance. First, it must be measurable. As in all scientific studies or comparable things, it must have a measurement to understand what constitutes success and failure. Secondly, it must be comparable to an existing standard. There must be some understood benchmark that our measurement fits into to define the performance. For example, batting average in baseball as compared to other hitters in the same division or level of competition, a quarterback rating in football against the rest of the league, etc. Thirdly, it must have consequences. If what you're doing doesn't matter in any way, then it is just an activity. This is where competition of performance can get confusing so let me clear the muddiness by giving an example we can all relate to. Who is that person that plays a game of monopoly, goes bowling with friends, or plays horseshoes at a family gathering and it becomes more about the score than the social interaction? We all have them in our lives so if you can't give the answer, just as in poker if you can't identify who the bad player is, you might want to ask your friends because it likely could be you.

The good news is that if it is you, you are now reading this book and can develop the skills to overcome the inherent desire to turn an activity into a competition with a false belief that you are performing some accomplishment to the delight of your ego and dismay of loved ones. Even at age 50, with all the experience and educational background I have, I still struggle in many events to remind myself that these are not competitive performances and that I need to understand the social implications of my behavior. The balance I have found is that there is no solution, only continued progress.

KEEP YOUR HEAD UP

We have all heard the expression, keep your head up. This is not usually a literal instruction, but rather a gentle reminder that things will get better. The funny irony of it is that this advice is usually given in times of adversity or defeat. I would contend that if this advice was given during times of triumph and great performances and given as a literal instruction it would be much more useful. Gaining confidence is difficult and maintaining a high level of confidence over time is even more challenging. Keeping your head up is a great source of confidence most useful before an event rather than after a loss.

Throughout my playing career, I heard phrases like "keep your head up," "show no fear," "be confident," and my favorite of all time, "just put it out of your mind." None of these slogans or phrases made me perform any better, but it did hurt the credibility of the person who said it to me because what in the hell do any of those mean? When someone says, "Be confident," it is about as effective as a pitching coach coming out to a struggling pitcher and saying, "Just throw strikes." Well, what does that pitching coach think the pitcher is trying to do, walk everyone?! Be assured that confidence comes from somewhere, but be equally assured it is not from slogans that have no meaning or substance.

Understanding where confidence comes from is the

launching point to building confidence. There are actually four specific areas that confidence comes from: personal experience, vicarious experience, self-talk, and body composition or the way we carry ourselves. Personal experience builds confidence because we have done it before so we are more apt to be successful in trying it again and with more practice, we know we will get better. This is most evident in watching an infant trying to learn to walk. While they may stumble and fall in the beginning, each new step builds confidence for future success. This example also illustrates that it is innate that we build confidence through trial and error, but that social pressures we learn later in life keep us from trying harder to succeed and often leads to giving up. The second source of confidence, vicarious experience, allows us to watch someone do something and learn from them. Whether someone does it better than us or not as well, we can gain a great amount of information to help improve our performance and build our confidence toward the skill we are trying to master. The third source of confidence, self-talk, is what we say to ourselves. Are our thoughts helping build our performance or are they getting in the way of our full potential? Self-talk can also be impacted from external sources. Think back to when you tried to do something for the first time that may have been difficult. Someone may have said, "You can't do that," or "What are you, crazy?" These external haters can start to impact our thoughts of what we believe our abilities to be. This is precisely why successful people surround themselves with other successful people. Finally, body posture is simply back to keeping your head up. It's standing tall, looking people in the eye, walking with a purpose, and standing your ground. I think of long-time Oriole's skipper, Earl Weaver. Short in stature but was a giant when confronting umpires. He did not slouch, drag his feet, or bow his head and had the uncanny ability to look eye to eye with someone six inches taller.

Having confidence is not an absence of doubt, but it does have the ability to mitigate those thoughts that could prevent us from performing at our optimal level. So, the next time someone tells you to have confidence, think about the various sources from where it comes. Either do it, watch someone do it, talk yourself into doing it, or carry yourself through it even when you may not know exactly what you are doing. I heard somewhere that anyone who is great at something was once a beginner. That is good advice to take whenever trying to attempt something new. Only through failure can we measure growth and understand mastery is a skill that takes time.

There are always opportunities to practice the skill of keeping your head up. Recently, I was conducting a class outside and it was cold and rainy. Something the brochure didn't show about South Carolina when I agreed to come here, but regardless we had the session and as the rain poured down, imagine if you would how most people carry themselves in the rain, head down and covered up. Instinctively, I saw this as an opportunity. I had everyone stand up and walk around with their head up, rain beating their faces, but we found that as I instructed them to keep their heads up facing the rain head on, several grunts turned to yells. Suddenly there they were, 185 trainees bellowing out in face of the freezing rain.

Toward the end of the exercise, the ridiculousness of it started to unfold and laughter began to seep from the moans and yells of incoherent phrases. It was at that moment that I realized, as did many of the trainees in the class, that our mood had changed, no longer focused on the dismal day that was presented, but rather our defiance in letting the conditions dictate how we would carry ourselves. Keeping your head up in moments of glory and pride is easy, keeping your head up in adversity is a necessary skill. The difference between defeat and opportunity is perspective and when perspective remains positive, the value of any measurement also changes.

THE MEASURE OF SUCCESS

Success is a term often associated with outcome. A successful hitter will be measured by his batting average, a successful salesperson makes a top earning for himself and his company, a successful quarterback has a certain completion percentage and quarterback rating, and a successful team is measured by the number of championships they win. While I do not want to discredit the metrics used in these areas, I do challenge the significance placed on them. The reason being is that when measurement of success is determined solely or primarily by the outcome, we take controllability out of the equation. So, if outcome is not the best measurement for success, what is?

Let us examine this a bit further by looking at the ignored metrics not figured into the outcome equation. For example, how much more batting practice does a player who hits .320 take over the player who hits .290? How many more meetings or hours worked does the successful salesperson make to meet or exceed the standard that another salesperson makes in just meeting the quota? How much more of a relationship does the quarterback make with his receivers that has the high quarterback rating? How much more teamwork does a team put into winning a championship than a team that just shows up for practice and games? Sometimes and unfortunately these variables are described as "intangibles" that players or teams have, but is that really true?

We hear the word intangible used by sports media often, and I think this is highly unfair to any athlete or performer. The Cambridge Dictionary defines *i*ntangible as "impossible to touch, to describe exactly, or to give an exact value." How insulting this must be to a player or team who puts in the effort to achieve greatness, to be their personal best. This is however the penalty we pay for looking at outcome measurements. When we look at a game in its entirety, we tend to give attention to uncontrollable factors such as a missed call by a referee or an umpire, the weather conditions, or even the venue in which the game was played. In the world of outcome measures we are constantly looking for excuses and what a discredit to elite athletes this is!

The truth is, the measure of success is in one word, effort. Effort may seem like an intangible but that is only because as a society we haven't taken time to measure it appropriately. Perhaps it is somewhat of an ambiguous term, but certainly it can become measurable with scientific data. We can measure VO^2 Max, we can measure verbal persuasion in the can do versus can't do words and phrases we use, we can measure it the swings we take in the cage, pitches we throw from the mound, the passes we make on the field, the call we make to follow up with a potential client. Effort, not intangibles, is what makes one player or performer better than another, but even more importantly than comparing against someone else, effort is what we measure to compete with ourselves to be our personal best.

Effort gets a bad rap, though. Honestly, it is not very sexy, and it does not make for good television commentary. We love to hear commentators say, "They rose to the occasion," "They played above their talent," or worse yet, "Luck was on their side." As the consumer where there is no emotional investment for us in a player or team, we love the underdog the media provides for us. We loved seeing the Cubs win its first World Series in over 100 years, we loved seeing Appalachian State beat Michigan, we loved seeing sixteen seed UMBC knock off favorite Virginia, we loved seeing Kirk Gibson hobble up to the plate and hit the game-winning home run in the 1988 World Series, and the entire world loved watching the Miracle on Ice. We love these moments in sports because they were not supposed to happen, because they lend us to feeling that anything is possible. What we were not told though and weren't privy to is the effort that those athletes and teams put in long before that moment or game happened.

Effort is boring most of the time, it is tedious, and it is done outside the view of most people. It is done in self-reflection. It is done in the solitude of the weight room. It is done on the practice field alone with no fanfare. But most importantly it is done so that intangibles do not. Effort provides controllability and controllability is the gateway of getting the desired outcome because focus is more directed and purposeful. Intangibles lead us to have the mindset that there are certain qualities that are either undefinable or uncontrollable and therefore just present themselves at unpredictable times.

I want to end this chapter with giving you some time to self-reflect and think about what you have previously perceived about outcome in sports and what you maybe thought about seeing the reactions of players on both sides. We have all witnessed the championship game where we see the celebrating team in tears of joy and the losing team in tears of defeat, but were those tears really about the win or loss of that game? Now I would speculate that maybe it was something else. I used to wonder how a team could lose game seven of a Stanley Cup and line up to shake hands with the opposing team moments after the final horn sounds. I used to wonder about college coaches who lost big games and talk primarily about the players they will miss after the season. I now wonder what you think.

PREPARING FOR GREATNESS

The first step toward greatness is just that, the first step. It's that thought that rises into a flame that becomes action. One of the best ways to take that step toward greatness is to let someone know about it. Telling someone makes you now accountable for the thing or things you said you would do. That is precisely what I did. In 2018, during a July family get-together at my parents' house in Ocean Pines, Maryland, I let Danny and Kelly know that I was going to attend the Orioles Dream Week with him.

I had just finished Grad School with a 4.0 and thought this would be the perfect opportunity to put all those sports psychology skills to beneficial use. Plus, it was as good an excuse as ever to convince Tara to shell out over four thousand dollars for Dream Week. It later became known as my "Gradubirthdayxmas" gift. That day, I went for a run and threw a ball around, took some swings, and was extremely excited and energized to get ready for this unprecedented challenge. The next two days I could hardly move. I knew I had to make a plan to get in baseball shape!

THE PLANNING PHASE

In the later part of the summer of 2018 after I made the announcement to my family, I knew there would only be a few months to get outside and throw before the cool October air and shorter days would take over. This was also the first time I had truly regretted moving from warm, sunny Arizona. That being said and with no time to waste, we constructed a pitching mound from Tara's design. This was a good plan since I was just going to pile dirt up into a makeshift mound. There was a statistical probability that my plan would have led to a broken ankle or worse. The design she created made it much more sturdy and professional looking. It even included bullpen benches that were already installed. The area was just over 75 feet long so I could set up a plate and net at the other end and start my bullpen sessions.

It took several days to get the ground level and mound built up, and at night, before the sun would go down, I'd take time to look out at its progress and think of my glory days of hurling fastballs and curveballs that would drop off the imaginary table. My motivation was stronger than ever to get back into competitive shape. By the end of the second week, now heading into the first part of August, the mound was complete.

With the planning phase of constructing the mound done,

the mental part of planning came into play. I decided to use an imagery script to go through both my stretching routine as well as my throwing routine. I replayed in my mind previous bullpen sessions from years ago but now incorporated more than just visualization. I used all my senses: the smell of the dirt, the sound of my cleats on the dirt, the taste of my fingers as I wet them, and the feel of the ball in my hand. I could feel the stitches of the ball as they meshed effortlessly into my index and middle finger; the ball held securely yet gently in my hand; feeling the ball rotate in my hand as it went from the grip of the fastball to the curve.

I would see myself delivering the first strike tailing to the outside corner away from a right-handed batter. I looked at myself both internally and from outside my body. From the inside I felt my body pivot and coil as my drive leg dropped slightly and my stride leg bent at the knee while my core became engaged and tightened. Then as I drive forward, I feel balanced and ready to drive in perfect concert to the plate, the breath exiting my body as I feel the torque in my arm propel the ball forward. I felt my front foot hit the front of the mound and the transfer of power from back to front, exploding into the release and follow through. I would then transition and view myself from the outside looking at my delivery, becoming a fan of my flawless mechanics.

In addition to pitching mechanics and the use of imagery, I developed a plan for conditioning as I knew summer would soon come to an end in the mountains of Tennessee where we lived. I purchased a stationary interactive bike to build endurance and had a weight station to use light weights.

I guess you could say that pitching is like riding a bike, once you get the muscle memory down you never forget it. The only difference with pitching is that there are more moving parts, and my parts were not moving quite the same way as they did the last time I pitched competitively some fifteen or more years ago. So, I started slowly for about a week and threw into the net from in front of the mound. I was even exceptionally good about going through my stretching routine that I recalled from many years ago, though much of the flexibility had abandoned my aging body.

Of course, as it is with many things, I quickly became bored with taking it slow and wanted to test out the new mound, so within a very short time I was back up towing the rubber. The plate and net that I had set up and measured precisely appeared farther than the sixty feet, six inches on my first few pitches as gravity seemed to bring the ball in shorter than I anticipated. After bouncing a few in the dirt, I was able to make some adjustments, slow my mechanics, and put the ball to the back of the netting. With this new mound in place, and my imagery fully engaged in practice, I wanted to take a couple of real throws from the mound. Tara agreed to video me throwing so that I could review my mechanics, so she took her place behind the net sitting on the ball bucket intently focused on me going into my deliberate rotation. What she was not focused on was her foot, on the edge of the netting. As I delivered a mighty fifty plus mile per hour heater to the net, it struck her foot; and in one pitch, I lost my videographer.

Eventually, I found an extra bag of topsoil and used that as my catcher and was able to mount my phone safely behind the bag to video my pitches and form. As I progressed in this practice of throwing, it was very gratifying to hear the thump of the ball hitting the bag and even greater satisfaction when I saw the bag start to give from the force of the ball. Though Tara, who had plans for that topsoil, did not express the same level of appreciation for my ability to spill the contents of the bag upon the ground.

Now that the planning phase was complete and I had all the equipment and mound in place, it was time to start seriously executing what I had on paper into action. This was going to be no small task as you will soon find out when my life was going to drastically change. By the middle of September, the countdown to Dream Week was on…time to get busy!

THE ACTION PHASE

In the middle of September, I took a trip to Ocean Pines where I visited my sister and nephew and for his twenty-first birthday. During the visit, I spoke with my sister about the expectations I had for my performance at Dream Week and made sure to do exercises daily while I was there. I ran in the mornings and, of course, had my glove and a couple of baseballs to run drills. One of the drills was the pick-up drill where I would place two balls about eight feet apart from each other and shuffle between the two picking up one, placing it down, shuffle to the other, pick it up and put it down and so on. Within a minute of doing this drill, I felt my quads burning and I was breathing heavy, but never let on the pain I was feeling.

Upon returning home, I continued to practice this drill and even did a YouTube video of stretching exercises that I shared with other Dream Week campers, setting the precedence that I would be an athlete prepared and ready to compete! When my brother-in-law, Danny, saw the video, the impression that I got was that he was less than excited. I was doing so much to prepare. He would tell me that it was really more for fun than anything and not to take it so seriously. This of course after showing me his championship ring from the year he had already gone, and his team won the championship. I later found out that he was on a nutrition plan and had been running on the treadmill.

Undeterred, I continued my daily regimen and pulled on my grad school experience to make sure I followed the goal setting plan I had set out for myself. That plan continued through October, and while I wasn't losing weight, I was getting in better physical condition and continued to throw off the mound four times a week, each outing becoming more on target with my pitches and increasing my pitch count. I had also made connections with a local indoor baseball camp who invited me to come and practice as often as I'd like. I was able to throw off their indoor mound on days of inclement weather and was even able to take some batting practice. Yes sir, the month of October was certainly going well!

Then came the month of November and with it a host of changes that would significantly impact my action phase and all this with just a little over two months to go before heading to Florida to compete in the Orioles Dream Week. In the first week of November, I was called about a job to work as a mental skills trainer with the Army. They offered me a position at Fort Stewart, Georgia, some six hours away from home, from my pitching mound, from my workout facility, and all the equipment I had in the den. Yes, indeed this was going to change things significantly.

ADAPT AND OVERCOME

While there were many challenges awaiting me in this new job, there were also many advantages. One great advantage was that the climate in Georgia was much milder so I would be able to train outside. Another advantage was that I would be working directly in the field that I had studied so my daily life would be surrounded with sport and performance in mind. All that being said, before I even arrived at Fort Stewart, I was going to have spent two weeks in mid-November in Washington, DC, for training and certification. I arrived in Washington on November 4th and would remain until November 17th. This meant that by the time I actually arrived in Georgia, it would be some time just after Thanksgiving, giving me considerably less time to train than initially planned before going to Florida for Dream Week. While possible to meet, it was certainly outside the parameters of what I had initially planned.

I did my best to work-out in the hotel gym where my

training took place in November. It was adequate for some cardio work and weights, but I desperately wanted to get out and throw. By the end of the certification process, I felt like my arm had become stagnant and was increasingly frustrated that all my work from the last few months was quickly vanishing. It was time to take stock in what I could control, and my return home could not have come at a better time.

The week of Thanksgiving I returned home to Bristol, Tennessee, where my workout area and pitching mound seemed to be held as if it were in a time capsule, awaiting my presence. It was as if the motivation still hung in the air and covered me as I walked in. As soon as I saw the environment I had created, I again regained focus and my motivation was fully intact. I had one week in my home environment before I had to move to Georgia and make a plan to continue my training for Dream Week, now just seven weeks away.

Once I arrived in Georgia, I found an apartment that did not provide much in terms of a spacious design like my house in Bristol, so I was at the mercy of the weather for any conditioning and training I wanted to do. In addition, I had to find a field that was both accessible and in good enough condition to throw and hit on. I was able to bring most of my gear with me that included a bucket of balls, my gloves, bats, cleats, tee, and home plate. What I did not have was my elliptical, stationary bike, or weights. After surveying the area and what my work schedule would consist of, I joined a Planet Fitness that provided the things I could not bring from home.

While I was getting into a good physical conditioning routine, I was concerned about not having anyone to play catch with. I would go to a local baseball field that remained flooded for the most part and long toss, but I could not quite measure the distance from the mound to the backstop and pitching against the backstop would end up ruining the bucket of baseballs I had so I decided to do what I did as a kid and find a rubber ball that I could throw against the wall of a makeshift outdoor racquetball court that was in my apartment complex. I thought back to the days before any arm problems, soreness, or fatigue and remembered that the way I improved was to just throw. Go outside and play and so that is what I did.

As I took the hard rubber ball and threw it against the wall of the outdoor court, it reminded me of playing as a child when I would take a pink rubber ball or a tennis ball and throw it against my front porch step. This time of play actually incorporated some particularly good skill sets that I did not fully appreciate at the time. I would go to the end of the walkway from my porch to a grassy area that separated the sidewalk from the curb. As I threw the ball toward the step, I had an exceedingly small margin for error. High and to the left was the living room glass panel window that overlooked the concrete porch. Missing to the right would land the ball in a thick rose bush full of thorns. Miss too low or two high on the two-step porch and the ball would ricochet off the screen door making a loud bang prompting a stern voice from inside from my mother to find somewhere else to throw the ball.

Of course, successful completion of a throw to the front porch was only half the skill of playing ball in the front yard alone. Once the ball returned , I had to field it without error or there too could be dire consequences. If the ball got directly past me and went into the street it could easily be directed into the storm sewer and be lost forever. Even if the ball didn't make it all the way to the storm sewer, we lived at the base of a large hill that once the ball made it to the street would take to the natural curve of the terrain and roll possibly up to a quarter of a mile before resting at the bottom of the neighborhood, that assuming that it wasn't pinned underneath a car tire along the way. As I returned my focus back to my current makeshift wall ball court, it amazed me that when I think of all the technology in the world today to measure ball spin, arm angles, and biomechanics nothing was quite as effective as the natural consequences of mom yelling at me or the thieving nature of a storm sewer to home in on my skill set of accuracy and concentration.

THE RACE

As December continued and I got more and more into my routine, the holidays certainly threw some metaphoric curveball into my training schedule. Trying to figure out when to travel back to Bristol and what the New Year's Eve festivities would consist of were all things to consider in the final stretch of preparation. As I looked for any opportunity to stay in training mode, I found an opportunity in a 5K Reindeer Run in Hinesville. I hadn't run a 5K for many, many years, but I figured that since I had been in training since mid-August surely, I could run a 5K.

Almost every day I have the opportunity to teach, instruct, or mentor and almost every day I talk about finding ways to grow from moments of failure. I explain that failure is almost expected when you step outside your comfort zone of accomplishments because you are taking a risk of some degree of uncertainty. I do all this very well in my sessions but practicing it myself can sometimes seem a much more daunting task. This was certainly the case for the 5K I ran. When I first arrived, it was a joyous and festive atmosphere just ten days before Christmas. Some people had those fake antlers on their head and some even went so far as to dress up in a Santa suit. Not me, though. Oh no, I was all business.

Weeks before when I initially signed up for the race, I went to Dick's Sporting Goods and bought a pretty expensive pair of running shoes, new socks, and long sleeve Under Armour sleek running top; and when I showed up, I was prepared to compete! As if I hadn't learned anything in my studies about performance and competition, I immediately began to size up others that were running. There were obviously some who were intrinsically motivated to run, but the vast majority I saw with a sense of contempt and uttered quietly to myself, "You can beat those fat asses." As shameful as I am to admit it, I think it is important to understand that though I have all the tools of mental skills training, I still sometimes stumble into the old trap of decompetition, a word I first heard coined by the late pioneering sports psychologist Terry Orlick.

As the horn sounded, I weaved my way around those poor bastards of trotters, walkers, and baby stroller pushers and found my groove and rhythm. I focused on my breathing and had my Spotify on with my Bluetooth wireless headphones each step-in sync with whatever inspirational song was playing. It was quite chilly, and I could see my breath with every exhale. Yes, sir, I could not be more pleased with myself...until. Yes, until that second mile. As I was running in stride, I observed a post in the ground that read, "One Mile," and I thought to myself that there had to be some calculated error. I looked at my watch at the nine-minute mark and could not fathom how I had traveled only such a short distance!

Suddenly, as if someone had stolen a lung from me, I felt winded, my side began to hurt, and that frigid air was now burning the inside of my throat. My legs began to stiffen, then turned to jello, the back to stiff again. I was losing control. At the halfway point, I saw runners in the distance begin to pass me in the opposite direction as they turned for home. *If this was a horse race*, I thought to myself, *you would have been shot*. Not put out to stud, not had monuments built, no, just shot. As if it couldn't get any worse, as I made the halfway point and turned back, I saw the stroller pushers gaining on me. I was fighting to stay out of last place. This was no longer a test of my conditioning and athletic competence. No, this was a fight for a trifle bit of dignity to not let the stroller pusher pass me. So, I fought, clawed, and used every motivational technique at my disposal to keep moving forward, to look ahead, to not think about stroller pusher getting past me and there it was, the finish line.

At long last, I conquered that Reindeer Run and survived the humiliation of being overtaken by, you guessed it, the baby stroller pusher. At thirty-two minutes and nineteen seconds, I did it. I took my reindeer medal, scooped up what little dignity and pride I had left, and made my way home with the realization that in less than five weeks, my competition was going to be somewhat better, and I was nowhere close to where I needed to be. In the last few days of the year, I needed to come up with a new plan, something to include a lot more cardio and a lot less beer. The one guiding hope was I knew that if Rocky could successfully train to fight Apollo Creed on such short notice, then I could do this. Despite me knowing that it was a fictional character and a fictional fight, I ignored that small detail in convincing myself of what I could achieve in a narrow amount of time. With this recent realization that I was ill prepared for the upcoming week's long competition I went back to work on conditioning and my throwing routine. I used all the mental skills I had learned and began to apply them. The entire time reminding myself of what Danny, my brother-in-law, had told me. It's just for fun. As I continued to progress in the days before heading back to Bristol for Christmas, I focused on the progress I had made. The fact that I actually completed the 5K run was more than I could have done prior to my regimen of training so with that I moved forward.

I returned to Georgia after several days at home in Tennessee, knowing I had now less than a month before Dream Week was to take place. Everything I did from here on out would be baseball related. I committed to going out to the baseball field at least three times a week and incorporating my wall ball training to just keep my arm steady and prepared to throw more than I had in over twenty years. I created my own practice plan as if I were a one-man team. I would go to the field and sit in the dugout, putting my cleats on and feeling the scrape of the cleats on the concrete of the dugout floor, smelling the dirt and grass enter my nasal passages, closing my eyes and feeling the sun on my face and the breeze of the cool southern winter air cool my cheeks and dry out my lips.

After taking several minutes to incorporate imagery, I would go out to the grass between the dugout and the infield and do my stretches for approximately twenty minutes before taking a lap around the entire field. Maintaining the sweat produced in the warmup, I would take my bucket of balls and throw short distance, long distance, then throw between thirty to forty-five pitches from the mound to my makeshift catcher which was a trash can turned on its side. I was fully integrating all my years of experience into the practice of playing the game I grew up loving and participating in the true dream of playing with and around my former big-league heroes from the Baltimore Orioles. I wanted and desired to engage fully in the experience and as the calendar turned over to 2019, my patience was fleeting and the reality of what I was about to experience filled my daily thoughts.

THE BATTING CAGES

In the early part of January, I received an email from the coordinator of Dream Week that there would be an opportunity for those participating to come to Camden Yards and take part in batting practice. With only twenty days to go, I decided to take the train from Georgia to Baltimore to have the opportunity to not only take batting practice in the indoor underground of Camden Yards, but also to meet other players that I would potentially be teammates of and those I would be competing against. I contacted Danny who informed me that when he did it last time, it was not for very long and that I may be wasting my time taking a long train ride for the event. Undeterred, I bought my train ticket and prepared for the eleven-hour train ride.

I left Savannah at around nine in the evening and arrived just after seven in the morning, and Danny picked me up to take me to Camden Yards. I was extremely excited on the train and that, combined with the lack of comfort in the seats, it was nearly impossible to sleep. Needless to say, while I was excited with anticipation, I was also very fatigued. As we arrived at the stadium, we were directed to the area for players entrance and down a long hallway that had large pictures of past Oriole greats on the walls. We made our way to the opposing locker room and were greeted by several of the Dream Week coordinators and some of the players that I would see again in just a couple of weeks. Some of the players were "rookies" like me who this was the first time, while the vast majority were veterans who had played in years past to include Danny. We were given our hitting groups and as I strapped on my batting gloves and awaited my turn, I took advantage of introducing myself to the other players. Danny and I even did a photoshoot in front of the MASN podium where so many press conferences were held. So many of late were disappointing press conferences, but that was a distant memory from this experience.

Finally, the letters of the alphabet included my name, and I made my way to the tunnel where the batting cages were. They had three cages set up with live pitching from behind an L screen. For those of you who are not familiar with baseball terminology, an L screen is simply a screen that the pitcher stands behind to protect himself from batted balls, and I was prepared to put on a pitch hitting exhibition. With great confidence from my months of preparation hitting off a tee, I knew I'd soon be experiencing the crack of the bat and all eyes a gaze on my hitting ability. I felt my energy begin to elevate as I got closer and closer to my turn. My hands began to sweat inside the batting gloves, my heart rate increased, and as I was well aware through my own clinics, I wanted to bring my energy back down to an acceptable level, so I took two, three, and then four deliberate breaths. I felt my heart rate return to an optimal level, my head clear, and I was entering my zone.

I stepped into the cage, beginning my showcase as a left-handed hitter. The first pitch was lobbed in and with a controlled, looping swing I threw my hands out, extending my arms, getting the head of the bat through the strike zone, but oddly felt nothing connected. All I heard was the thump of the ball hitting the pad in the back of the cage. Oh no, I thought…I whiffed! The second pitch was a dismal foul ball that I barely connected with. Then the pitcher said, "Ok, eight more." What! wait a minute! Ten pitches were all I was going to see. I immediately switched to a right-handed batting stance and connected on the next pitch, a little bit better on the following, but then, just as I was getting into my groove, it was over.

I returned to the locker room and asked Danny quietly, as to not give away my rookie status and inept knowledge of how this day was supposed to go, "When will I get to go back and have another attempt?" He responded with two simple words, "That's it." In nearly a state of shock I could only respond, "Oh." I took off my batting gloves, picked up my bat, and headed back toward Danny's car. By 11:00 a.m., it was all over.

Determined to get the most out of this trip, I decided to have Danny take me to Play it Again Sports, a chain store that had used equipment. I saw a huge baseball bag, enough to fit all the equipment I ever owned since I started playing baseball. This gave me an idea though that would allow me to leave with more than I came with. It may have been sleep deprivation or just the idea that I had to get something more out of this trip, but I decided to get the bag and then two cases of Natty Boh, a local beer used more for steaming crabs rather than drinking it while eating them. Regardless, it was something that I could not get outside of Maryland, and I wanted some to take home with me. So, with my two cases of beer, baseball gear, and the change of clothes I brought with me, I packed up and headed back to the station for the departing train that would get me back to Georgia sometime in the early morning of the next day.

My nephew Kevin, drove me to the train station. As I approached the ticket counter, I told them I wanted to check my newly purchased baseball bag into checked baggage. With the equipment and two cases of beer, it weighed about sixty pounds.

As the attendant put the bag on the scale, he heard the bottles clanking around inside the bag. He informed me that I was neither able to check the bag with said beer in it, nor take it on the train as a carry-on. It occurred to me that my well-thought-out plan had not survived the action phase so well. I was determined to get the bag and all its contents onto that train. With that, I retrieved the bag and began lugging it around Penn Station waiting for my train that was still two hours from departure.

Eventually, the time came to board the train and being there so early I was one of the first in line. Again, not a very well-managed plan. Having this bulky and heavy bag and being first in line, I had to somehow manage to get this protuberant object to fit in the narrow overhead area for storage bags. As I struggled, no one assisted me, instead letting out moans that reflected disgust and disapproval of my clandestine operation to smuggle local beer to Georgia. Finally, as if I was Atlas carrying the world, I placed the bag on my shoulders, up to my head, and with determination hoisted the bag into the compartment. By this time, it was clear, no one would want to sit next to me which was fine.

THE FINAL PUSH

After returning home from my combined 22-hour train ride for ten swings in the batting cage, I knew it was time to start hitting the throwing routine hard. My plan was to do just as I had done when I pitched in my younger days. With fourteen days to go before I left for Florida, I would divide those up into three starts. Day one I would long toss; day two I would throw a thirty-pitch bullpen session; day three I would jog the outfield and then throw another thirty pitches; day four I would do my exact pre-performance pitching routine, stretches, warm up, and then seventy pitches from the mound. That would give me three full rotations with two days off in between. It was a great plan with realistic execution.

If you have not learned from my previous experiences, my plans almost always need some adjusting. After the second round of my workout routine, I felt something. It was a slight tingling in my elbow and an almost heavy feeling in my bicep. It was undoubtedly not a good sign with only eight days to go! Of course, this was not my first time experiencing such feelings, and I knew exactly what I needed to do…a cortisone shot. I scheduled an appointment with a physical therapist who gave me the injection and the idea to use KT Tape to keep my shoulder in place as I still needed to continue to throw. The second day after the injection with the tape in place, I returned to the mound and backed off to forty-five pitches, but the floating thought of an injury so close to Dream Week was a horror I could not even comprehend. Whenever a thought of illness or injury would enter my mind, I used all my training and knowledge about sport and performance psychology to change my thoughts toward anticipation and the success of optimal performance in competition. In the last nine months, I had done all I could do. It was time to go to Dream Week and toe the rubber like I had not done in twenty-one years. The countdown was over, and with that, I packed my bags and headed for Sarasota.

PART TWO
THE EXPERIENCE BEGINS

THE ARRIVAL

THE DRIVE DOWN

It was January 25th, 2019, and I was heading down to Florida leaving mid-day. I was planning to stop about halfway and spend the night since the majority of other players/campers who still resided in Baltimore were not arriving on a flight until the 27th. I also wanted to arrive early and have my car parked at the facility, so no one there knew I had a car. I did not want to be everyone's taxi service when it was discovered that I was one of the few people there who had their own vehicle. I also knew that there was a thirty-minute shuttle from the resort to the ball fields, but again, I wanted to have my own transportation, to come and go as I pleased.

As I was driving down the highway, I started to reminisce about all the teams I had played for and the many incredible memories I had as a pitcher in baseball, college and beyond. I started to think of the friends I had made and their unique qualities that made them unforgettable. I thought about how amazing this experience was going to be and how jealous all those old teammates might be, knowing I that was going to be hobnobbing with some of the greatest Orioles and baseball players to ever play the game. I made a few phone calls to old teammates that though we were Facebook friends, we had not really spoken in a decade or more. I had a conversation with one of my former teammates who expressed his jealousy quite candidly but also said he was living vicariously through my personal experience. We spoke for over an hour, and before I knew it the first three hours of my six-hour journey to Sarasota was nearly done.

As I scouted the area, I saw the city of Ocala on the map and decided to stop there for the evening. As I entered the room of the Days Inn, it brought back so many memories of road trips I had taken as a player in college in the independent league. I remember as a senior and team captain in college back in the day, where hazing was still acceptable, we all stayed at Days Inn and were relentless on the freshman. There was this one time that we were on a road trip in Virginia in early March, so the weather was still very chilly and dipped into the lower 40's at night. One night we thought it a clever idea to take some of the freshman's bags to the outdoor pool. We told them that we would throw their bags in the pool if they did not jump in before we counted down from thirty. No bags were thrown into the pool, but I cannot confirm or deny that several freshman players got pneumonia.

Another road trip that did not involve hazing but did involve a memorable scenario was when I played for Salisbury University. We were somewhere in Virginia again, this time heading to Florida and playing several non-conference games when our bus broke down. When we awoke in the morning, our coach told us to take our equipment bags out of the bus trailer and to change into our uniforms. So, there we were with nothing but our equipment bags and the uniforms we had on our back. We sat there on the curb waiting anxiously to see what was going to happen next as our bus was towed off into the distance by the most Bubba of Bubba's to ever be given that name.

As we sat there looking at each other, no other coaches in sight, we began to wonder if we would make it to our next double header or the tournament in Florida we were ultimately heading for. After about a half hour, four sedan-style cars pulled up, and there are our coaches stepping out of them. They told us to put our bags in the trunk and pile in. Three in the back seat and two in the front. So, we did as instructed but there still remained five players not able to get into any of the fully-packed cars. Suddenly, we heard our head coach start to count out loud, "Six, nine, twelve, nineteen...goddammit...we need another vehicle!" Clearly, when the coaches determined how many cars we needed to get our players to the next game, they didn't take into account themselves as the drivers.

In an expletive-laced tangent, the head coach threw down his ball cap on the ground, and from inside the car I could see him start counting to five of the players, two pitchers from the game yesterday and three other players who never started for us. It was clear that the "no man left behind" slogan was not part of our team motto. Our coach instructed them to stay with the bus driver and they would catch up with us later that evening in North Carolina after the team bus had been repaired. That sounded like a legitimate plan at the time. So off we caravanned to our next double header in Smithfield, North Carolina.

We made it just in time to not have the game forfeited, but due to the travel accommodations and no time for batting practice or infield/outfield drills, we were absolutely destroyed in both games. I did not get to pitch in either game. That evening we realized suddenly that as we shared four rooms, none of us had our personal bags. No toothbrush, deodorant, clean change of underwear, or clean uniforms. We had only what we carried in our equipment bags and the uniforms we wore for the games —the double-header games where most players were dirty and sweaty. That was it. To make matters worse, the coach had also left his personal bag with his wallet and the team's meal money and other allowances in it. You have to understand that this was the early 1990's and ATM machines were not available on every street corner. There was no PayPal, Venmo, or Google Pay. There was whatever change or few dollars we had in our bags. It was okay though; we could survive one night until the team bus and trailer caught up with us.

The next morning, we all awoke to the stench of ourselves and our teammates. We were sure we would be greeted in the parking lot with the team bus and trailer in tow, but to our surprise, there was no team bus. Even the cars had been returned to the rental company. All that was in the parking lot was a shuttle bus like someone would take to the airport. Knowing there were no airports in the areas where we were playing games, it seemed unlikely that we were flying anywhere and even more unlikely that we may ever see our possessions again. As if things could not get any worse, our head coach came with two boxes of Power Bars and informed us to each take two, one for breakfast and one for lunch. He assured us that by dinner our team bus would catch up to where we were, but doubt of that was beginning to creep into all our minds. So, with our two Power Bars distributed, we set off to our next game in an unknown place in deeper North Carolina.

This second set of double headers concluded much like the day before. I do not remember the score, but I do remember as with the day before I did not get into either game. Not only was I hungry, tired, and dirty (though not as dirty as most who played), I was not even called upon to pitch. As we made our way to the next hotel, we were told that the team bus was still a day behind us. The good news is that the University had wired some money to the head coach, so at least we would get a full meal. We got to eat at a buffet and I am sure that those who were there had never before or since seen such a savage bunch of baseball players in their lives.

When we got back to the hotel, we settled into our rooms and took the useless showers before getting back into our now three-day underwear, socks, and uniforms. Suddenly, a loud knock was at our door, and we could hear our head coach stirring up an almost incomprehensible string of curse words, "Jeez us ka rights, open this gawd damn door!" As one of us opened the door he came barreling through, almost running over us while exclaiming, "I'm hiding in yous all bathroom and for flocks sakes don't open that sum bash for nobody!" Later, we found out that Coach was going from room to room hiding from the parents of one of the players we left behind in Virginia three days ago. Apparently, he had been arrested. We later found out that the bus driver had taken the five players that did not go with us to a strip club, and he and the underage minors were arrested and detained. That apparently was the reason the team bus had not caught up with us. It was only after the eighteen-year-old freshman called his parents for bail money that the whole thing came crashing down. The parents then were looking for our head coach for an explanation that he was obviously trying to avoid giving. The next day the team bus arrived, minus one bench player whose parents decided to have him transfer to another school.

As I sat on the edge of my bed thinking about the past, it occurred to me that it was literally a half a lifetime ago. It was hard to imagine that at nearly fifty years old I did not see myself as old as I should when I was twenty-five. I often get into conversations with people today who are in their fifties as I now am about how old we actually are, and they often counter with fifty is not that old. I have a pretty recallable memory that when I was twenty-five, fifty was old to me. I guess like most things in life, it is all about perspective.

It was not long into my deep contemplation that I realized that my fifty-year-old ass was getting hungry, so I went to a local Mexican restaurant that had extremely large margaritas. After eating and drinking a couple of those margaritas I found that I was feeling more youthful and caught my second wind. I decided to go down the street to a makeshift night club where neon lights and loud music drew my attention from a block away. As I made my way inside, I was pleasantly surprised that the average age was at least in the mid-thirties, so I did not feel so out of place. I also knew that the more I had to drink the younger I would continue to feel, at least until the sun came up.

There were obviously several things that were vastly different about this road trip than when I played baseball in my twenties. First, my tolerance for a hangover had significantly declined over the years, and secondly, I was married, so the exploits I recall from my "playing" days would not be acceptable now. That said, I learned quickly that wearing a wedding band does not deter women from approaching a married man. At least not as it applied in my situation. Another interesting fact I have learned is that an attitude can be sensed by a woman. If I was desperately looking for a woman, I would have not been approached by anyone, but the fact that I was sitting comfortably, confidently, and alone sipping my whiskey definitely created a curiosity about me. Of course, me being an Irishman in a bar set the atmosphere for me to do some of my best story telling. And the fact that I was on my way to play in a professional baseball arena certainly enhanced my role and ability.

As the night went on and I had three or four conversations with different people from the local area, I enjoyed watching people interact and could not feel a bit superior to their existence knowing what tomorrow was going to bring for me. Finally, the last call was made and my nostalgic evening of being a ball player out on the town during a road trip came to an end. As I made my way back to the hotel, thoughts of previous nights when I was with teammates started to come to mind, and I laughed at some of the things we did and the ladies we romanced being the elite athletes we believed we were at the time. I will claim these as innocent times, but just as adamantly state that I am extremely grateful that there was no social media at the time or recording devices at our fingertips. Such technology would probably have excluded me from many of the public trust positions I have held over the years.

As I turned in for the night, I let my thoughts take me to the upcoming day ahead which would land me in Sarasota a full day ahead of the other campers. I had no idea what to expect but thought maybe they might have a mound I could pitch from or at least a batting cage that I could take some early swings. I was aware that the day everyone else arrived there would be a tryout and then a subsequent draft. I had to make sure my stock value remained high and that I was as prepared as possible. Even though there were constant reminders from Danny and emails from the coordinators of the week that it was all about having fun and staying healthy, I also knew that anyone that would be holding a draft would also be looking at the competition factor.

The next morning on the 26th of January, waking up full of anticipation and unable to sleep any longer, I decided to get up and get an early start. Being that Sarasota was only a couple hours away, I took my time, got something to eat, and hit the road. I arrived at the Orioles minor league facility shortly after noon and parked my car. I walked up to the front entrance and quietly made my way inside. The lights were on, and I could hear voices in the distance, but no one was easily seen. I thought to myself that I may get detained and kicked out before I ever get to experience day one of anything.

FIRST IMPRESSIONS

Not knowing where I was going, I started walking around and came across a gym that had weights, ellipticals, bikes, everything needed to stretch and get game ready. Eventually, I saw someone walking my way with an inquisitive look despite my being dressed in an Orioles cap and old college baseball windbreaker. Before he could ascertain who I was, I confidently asked as if I was a regular at the facility, "Hey, good afternoon, do you know where I can find Steve?" I remembered his name from the numerous emails he sent us to help us prepare for the upcoming week. I had also met him at Camden Yards a couple of weeks ago during my batting practice train ride saga.

He directed me down a hallway to the office where sitting behind a desk piled with baseballs and souvenir trinkets was the friendly face of Steve. I introduced myself, and he warmly welcomed me. He gave me a packet of information to include the hotel we would be staying at and who my roommate would be. This was starting to feel like a real spring training already, being roomed with a complete stranger. In case you are wondering why I did not room with Danny, it was because my sister was accompanying him and participating in some of the events. Of course, she did not dress in uniform and play; there would not be enough therapy in the world to erase that image from my brain. She was there to meet the players and players' wives, go to dinners, and pretty much just socialize. Since Tara did not know any of the Orioles and was not really a baseball fan, the few thousand dollars more was not worth it to her to take the trip, so I was solo, but each room had to have two players per occupying it.

After giving me the basic rundown, Steve asked if I would like to tour the facility since the majority of campers were not going to arrive until the morrow, and he did not have much else to do. He let me know that I would be able to check into my room that evening and then took me to the locker room area that had names on every locker. I roamed up and down the aisles and finally found the locker that had my name on it. I was a little taken aback that they had put my name as John Quinn instead of J.P., but I guess I could live with it for the time being. I did bring the mistake to Steve's attention. He said they would gladly order one with my correct name, but it may not arrive before the end of the week.

I then made my way into the shower area that had enough sinks it seemed to give each player his own personal area. On the counters were all the necessities to wash and groom oneself to include not only soap and shampoo, but razors, shaving cream, and even suntan lotion. Just outside each entry to the bathroom were giant tubs which I could not determine at the time what they would be used for but was sure I would find out in the upcoming days. Beyond the locker room was the training area. I met one of the trainers who was preparing for the upcoming week. He joked how this area was like the calm before the storm. I assured him that while I would seek out their services prior to pitching a game that I had been conditioning myself for months and was ready to endure all that the week had ahead. He laughed and replied with, "We'll see."

After touring the building, I decided to take a walk around the fields where we would be playing our games and see what kind of shape they were in since we were reporting weeks ahead of spring training. As I made my way down the sidewalk, I noticed a couple of guys throwing in the outfield. They asked if I had my glove and wanted to play catch. I gathered from their age and appearance that they were most likely campers that arrived early as had I. Two of them confirmed that they were returning players from previous years and would help me settle in and get used to the routine. After about a half hour of playing catch, it started to rain so we made our way back to the facility, and I decided to head to the hotel and get checked in.

So far everyone was extremely pleasant and helpful, which I was grateful for since I did not really know what kind of people I would encounter. I got directions to the resort where we would be staying, and to my surprise it was thirty minutes away. I decided that I would drive my car to the field the next day but then might take the bus depending on how early we had to get up. As I arrived at the hotel lobby, there were a few people already checked in that were not traveling with the charter flight from Baltimore. It was there that I first came across someone who I had no idea what our week and journey would entail.

I first saw him in the lobby of the hotel. He was wearing an

Orioles hat and a raggedy shirt with a shark tooth necklace. While I suspected he was there for the Dream Week, he certainly looked too tan and hip to be from Baltimore. I was wearing my Orioles hat and a Tennessee baseball shirt that was matching the orange and black scheme of my hat. He approached me and asked if I had any idea what we were supposed to do or where we were supposed to report. He told me his name was Patrick, and though I am horrible at remembering names, this one would be easy since it was my middle name. He told me he was from California and just flew in. We made a few more pleasantries before checking in and heading to our rooms.

The next morning, I saw Patrick again in the lobby. I told him that I had a car, and he was free to ride in with me to the ballpark, but he let me know that he was taking the shuttle bus. We needed to report by eleven in the morning as those who were flying in would be arriving all around that time. I did know from talking to Danny that the first day we would meet at the clubhouse and have an introduction and then we would suit up for tryouts and assessments. When I arrived at the clubhouse, I knew exactly where to go since I had been there the day before. This time, however, when I arrived at my locker it was now filled with my uniform and an Orioles bag. I later would find out that they gave us a gift in our lockers each day when we arrived.

Shortly after changing into my uniform, I saw Patrick arrive. His locker was at the end of the row next to mine. We began talking and at some point, he made a Seinfeld reference. This would be the bond that would strengthen our relationship as the week went on. Patrick was laid back but also had a charismatic energy about him, laughing at the most obscure things. I also appreciated this about him as I, too, often find humor in small, yet obvious details. Oftentimes we would find that we would be laughing at the expense of someone who was oblivious at whatever character trait we detected. Soon others began to arrive and come into the locker room. It quickly became clear who were returning players and who, like Patrick and I, were the rookies in the camp.

Eventually, announcements began to come in that we were all to meet in the cafeteria for our orientation and expectations of the week. The first point of topic was how to use a string to attach our uniforms at the end of the day so they could be laundered and then hung up the next day for our upcoming games. We were provided one pair of pants, one hat, one pair of sanitary socks and one home jersey that was white and one away jersey that was black. Because of my distinguished mid-section, I was desperately hoping we would be the away team for most of the games as I always felt I looked better in black. We were also told that due to the rain from the previous day as well as the showers that continued off and on, that the fields were not in playable condition, so the typical tryouts were going to be adjusted to indoor batting cages and a few pitching mounds.

After the initial orientation, we were told that the rest of the afternoon would be spent with the former pros who would evaluate us hitting and throwing. We were also encouraged not to ask for autographs but to enjoy the experience of just playing baseball and getting their instruction. After that, we would be taking photos in the outfield grass that would eventually be sold to us for our baseball cards at a later date by the professional photographers that were there. Finally, we would head back to the resort and attend an introductory banquet where we could mingle with the pros. Then a draft would be held, and I would know which team I was going to play on. I wore the number sixteen on my jersey as I did in high school as my idol Scott McGregor had when he played for the Orioles. I wanted nothing more than to be on his team from the moment I had signed up many months ago. I also wasn't sure if I would be on Danny's team or not as I had not requested that specifically, though I found out later that Danny had. While it did not matter to me at the time, it created nice memories that we have shared since and as always Danny provided exceptional stories that will come later.

So, I made my way to the far end of the fields where there was an indoor facility that housed approximately five batting cages and three mounds. I decided to get my swings in first. Unlike the switch-hitting display I intended to put on a few weeks earlier at the Camden Yards batting cages I abandoned any notion of trying to hit left-handed and stuck to what I knew best and took my turn in the right-handed batter's box. When I got in, I was amazed to see that former Oriole great Al Bumbry was tossing batting practice in the cage. It was a surreal experience and took me a few swings to be able to concentrate on what I was doing. As I struck the ball a few times, Bumbry, also known as the Bumble Bee, gave me some minor pointers and immediately I was driving the ball up the middle. Every crack of the bat, I was gaining more and more confidence; and I had not even shown off my greatest strength yet, my pitching.

After taking a few more rounds in the cage I moved down to the end where the pitching mounds were. I was looking for Scott McGregor to be watching, but he was standing just to the outside of the batting area. I had worked on my mechanics to match his delivery as close as I could. From the wind up I would take a small step back, then pivot onto my left foot and then drive toward home plate dropping both arms below my right knee and coming through with a three-quarter delivery just like I had seen him do on the videos I studied of him pitching as well as still pictures that I had put in sequential order. Yes sir, I was almost a mirror image of my childhood and adolescent hero. My brother-in-law, Danny, was catching me at the other end. I directed him inside and outside, mastering my location with my fastball and curve. The indoor facility provided an echo that made my sixty mile an hour heater sound ninety. I would throw a fastball and "POP" you would hear it hit the mitt. Eventually I started to draw the attention of some of the pros who would be drafting players later that afternoon when all of a sudden, I heard a bellowing voice say, "Quinn, you got a phone call!"

As I turned around, there was the intimidating Jeff Tackett. He was only a few years older than me and played professionally the same time I was playing college baseball. I turned back around and threw a couple more pitches still hoping to catch the attention of Scott McGregor when Tackett repeated his demand that I take a phone call, this time with more conviction and a few expletives. Danny and I laughed at the suggestion that I not throw any more pitches. I could only hope now that I had done enough to impress upon the coaches to take me in one of the early rounds. As the workout concluded, I began to assess other players that I would soon be competing against. I had lost track of Patrick but knew I would see him later at the banquet that evening. I walked back into the clubhouse and locker room and that was when I discovered the use for those big tubs I had seen the day before. They were full of ice-cold beer. Miller, Bud, and Coors. There were several tubs all full of hundreds of cans to choose from. In the cafeteria they had provided us with cold cut subs and potato chips on our first day. In the orientation we were informed that breakfast would be held during the morning meetings at seven in the morning. That meant we had to be on the bus by six. I had the feeling that this was going to be a whirlwind of a week and that I would have to just go with it and soak it all in as we went. I also decided that my car would remain at the facility, and I would take the bus to and from the resort with the other players.

As I finished my sub and chips, I grabbed a beer to go and as I was walking out, I came across Patrick who was also leaving at the same time. On the ride back, we discussed our performance and quietly whispered that someone was going to have females on the team. Neither of us said it aloud, but we both were thinking the same thing—we wanted no girls on our team. Patrick asked about what positions I was going to play, and it occurred to me that I have been exclusively a pitcher since high school and had no idea what else I might want to play. I no longer had the range for outfield and being a lefty, it was not practical that I would play infield except for first base. Patrick said that he never really pitched and that he expected that most of his time would be at shortstop. We both thought how great it would be if we could be on the same team, me on the hill and him plugging up the middle.

After the half hour ride, we parted ways and prepared for the banquet dinner and draft. I was anxiously awaiting the results and to see how far up the order I would make it. As I made my way to the banquet room, there was an open bar on the outside which again called my name. As I was standing there getting my whiskey, I looked over my shoulder and there was Greg Olsen, one of the greatest Orioles relievers of all time. I could hardly recall much of his playing career but did remember that he came on board during the worst season the Orioles started off with to date and then was full time for the "why not" year where the Orioles were unlikely contenders. I was not sure I would be able to get used to seeing these past Orioles greats that I spent watching during some of my best years playing as well. The games had not yet begun, and it was already better than I could have ever imagined.

With my drink I headed into the large banquet room of the resort where we were all staying. Upon entering, I saw Kelly and Danny at one of the tables sitting with other players who played when Danny was part of the championship team two years prior. I am typically terrible at recognizing faces of famous people, so I was asking both of them who some of the former pros were that clearly were the center of conversations with small masses of people surrounding them. I am, in fact, so bad at facial recognition that once when I was playing a tournament at the World Series of Poker at the Rio, I saw two people at the rail watching our table. I turned to the player next to me and indicated that while they did look familiar, I had no idea who it was. The player looked at me in complete disbelief and informed me that it was, in fact, Phil Jackson and Lebron James. There were other celebrities and professional poker players over the years that I have come in contact with and spoken to that I had no idea who they were until someone else brought it to my attention. So, to say I would be a terrible eyewitness is an understatement.

As I scanned the room and saw some faces that looked recognizable, there was one that stood out and was no doubt. It was Scott McGregor. I introduced myself and reminisced with him about a time when I was about to play a game in my summer league, and he was there coaching a team on another field when he asked if he could borrow my glove to throw batting practice. To no surprise, he did not recall the event as vividly as I. There were so many questions I wanted to ask him, but one that applied specifically to my field of sport and performance psychology was to know what he was thinking as he pitched in that final inning of the 1983 World Series. I wondered if he was thinking about winning the game, one hitter at a time, the impending celebration, the immortality, and his answer was just what one may think of a successful elite athlete in a high-pressure situation. He simply said he was focused on making his pitch, each pitch, one at a time.

After taking up probably more time than I deserved with Scott, yes, we were on a first name basis after our interaction, I made my way through the room. I had pictures taken with several of the former Oriole players including Scott, Chris Hoiles, Rich Dauer, and Josh Towers who looked like he stepped right out of *GQ* magazine. As the conversations and whiskey flowed, I was feeling more at ease and comfortable. Then after our buffet style dinner, it was time for the draft. It didn't take long before my name was called, and I was drafted to Devo's Desperados. I found out later that any player who had a friend or relative at the camp would be drafted together so if one was drafted early and the other one followed then that team would lose a pick in the next round. I assumed that I was the early pick and Danny was along for the ride, but he believed just the opposite since he had already been part of a team that won the championship. Despite my probing throughout the week to the coaches, Mike Devereaux and Ross Grimsley, I could never confirm who was actually that first round pick. As the team came together, one of my worst initial concerns came true. Two of the females that came together were also selected on our team. Once again, I tried to convince myself that this experience was designed to be a fun-filled, fan-friendly week of playing baseball, but my competitiveness still wanted to compare rosters to who I thought would be a contender. Overall, I think there were a total of eight females that were playing and while I still had my reservations, I was sure that the overall skill level of the majority of players would not match my knowledge and ability.

While looking at the team as we stood up in the front of the room being introduced, a memory came to me of the last time I played on a team with Danny. I was playing a double header at a baseball field during one of my summer leagues in college, and Danny had a softball team he played on that was playing across the street at the softball complex. I remember that I pitched five innings in one of the games and three innings in the second game. After the baseball games concluded, I went over to the softball fields to watch Danny play. When I arrived, he told me that they only had eight players and needed at least nine to compete and asked if I would play in centerfield for their team. He told me to cover as much ground as I could because the guy they had in right field was no good. Being that I was a fairly good athlete (my one attempt at modesty here) at the time, I figured a softball game would be no problem, and it was exciting to think I would get to hit, as well. Being a pitcher in baseball, I never got to hit being they always had a designated hitter wherever I played, so I agreed.

It was the first inning, and we were the home team, so we had to play in the field first. The first couple of batters got on from infield hits, or bobbles is more like it. It suddenly occurred to me that the players on this team were not very good and were primarily there for socialization and the inevitable trip to the bar afterward. With two men on the bases and no one out, I looked at the runner on second base and knew if anything was hit to me, I could definitely throw him out at the plate. Then it happened. A fly ball directly to right field, right at the guy playing the position. All he had to do was take a few steps in and catch the ball as he was unwittingly in perfect position.

As I jogged over, I saw him flutter back, then forward, his arm fully extended out as if he was reaching high up into the heavens and my jog turned into a full sprint under the impression that without divine intervention there was no way he was going to catch that ball. As my footsteps approached, he glanced in my direction for a split second before I yelled, "Catch it!" The ball arched down from the clear blue sky, traveled right over the top of his glove and smacked him right in the face. Tending to the priority at hand, I pushed him off the ball that had rested underneath him and threw it into second base, blood spiraling off the ball as it rotated through the air. His nose broken and unable to continue, we were forced to forfeit the game and that ended my brief moment of time I had ever played on Danny's team. I could only hope with twelve players we would not have such an unfortunate experience this time.

As all the ten teams were drafted with twelve players per team, we eventually congregated around the table together and did some quick introductions. It had been a long day, especially for those who had flown in that morning, so we agreed to meet early in the cafeteria the next day to better learn about one another. As we headed out, some of the players and other former pros planned a nightcap meeting in the bar downstairs. I met up with Patrick who had been drafted to Gulliver's Travelers and would have Glenn Gulliver and Gregg Olson as their coaches. He felt like they had a good group from what he could tell, and we toasted to the upcoming week and hopefully facing off in the championship game against each other. We sat at the bar and listened to some of the former pros tell stories of the days they played and for those of them who were on that World Series team talk about that season and being champions. Some were even wearing their World Series rings. It was quite the first day and evening, but now it was time to get to bed. When I returned to my room, my roommate was already asleep, so I quietly made my way in and found myself easily dozing off in spite of the level of excitement and anticipation of what was to come.

EXCELLENCE BEYOND WINNING

At 6:00 a.m. the alarm went off and I jumped in the shower, got dressed, and was in the lobby of the resort by 0620 ready to catch the first bus. It was a chilly morning, and I could tell it was raining again. As I stepped onto the team bus, I thought back to many memories of doing the same thing. I wore shorts over my slider shorts, my sanitary socks pulled up over my calves, and an Orioles beanie cap. About the only thing different from when I played before was that my Walkman was replaced with Spotify and much better earbuds.

As the bus pulled off, there was that familiar feeling of a road trip, and many memories started to come to mind that I had not thought about in years. I remember one time riding on the team bus back from a game against Bluefield that we lost badly in a game that I thankfully had no part in. Some of us were talking and joking around when suddenly the bus pulled off onto the shoulder and our coach began screaming at us to "run up the mountain!" If you have ever driven through Bluefield, West Virginia, then you will undoubtedly recall the tunnels through the mountains. Well, it was precisely coming out of one of those tunnels that our coach decided to discipline us for the loss and complacency we apparently demonstrated on the ride home. So, there we were in our shorts and flip flops or tennis shoes running up the side of this recently snow-covered mountain, not hill, mountain. Of course, the majority of our bus rides were less punitive and much more enjoyable, but all were memorable.

As I returned consciousness back to my present situation, I chose not to socialize on the bus ride that first day, not because I was concerned about the bus driver pulling over and making me run a nonexistent snow-covered mountain, but I wanted to focus on my upcoming pitching performance and who we might be playing against. So, I sat back and began doing some imagery on the way in. I started with my earbuds in and listened to some pumped-up high-energy music, but as I settled into the imagery script in my head, the sound of the music faded to the background, then the humming of the bus engine came and faded. The sensations of my breath came into the foreground of awareness as did the feeling of my body sitting into the chair. As I transitioned myself through imagery to the field of play, I could feel the cleats on the soft surface of the outfield grass as I threw with Danny, feeling the sensations of the ball in my hand, the stitches of the ball flowing evenly and effortlessly across my fingers as I released it. Watching it sail through the air and into the recipient's mitt.

As I see myself finish warming up, I walk to the dugout area. I feel the sun on my face and the warmth of the air go across my cheek. With every stride, I feel the muscles in my legs oppositely relax and contract. I feel completely balanced. I hear the sound of other players talking and playing catch in the background. I feel the transition from the grass to the concrete of the dugout. I hear my cleats as they make contact with the foundation of the dugout. I can feel a bead of sweat drip from my forehead to my lips. I take a drink of water and feel the coolness enter my mouth and slide down my throat, cooling my body. Then the brakes of the bus come into the foreground of my mind, and the shifting of weight brings me back to the present moment as the bus pulls up to the entrance of the clubhouse.

WHEN THE FANS GO HOME

I grab my small bag of items and make my way to the locker room that is silent and calm as we are the first, other than the clubhouse staff, to arrive at the facility. In the back room, we can hear the trainers pouring ice and setting up stations for the weary campers who are about to embark on their first day. Slowly but surely, the other buses arrive; and within a short amount of time, there is rumbling throughout the locker room. I was not aware prior to this moment that the former pros would be dressing in the same locker room as the campers, which gave it more of a big-league feel. I put on my sanitary socks and left my shorts on as I would have done back in my playing days knowing I would have time to put on the full uniform prior to going to the field. I reintroduced myself to some of the fellow veteran campers that I met the night prior as well as Danny and some of the players drafted to Devo's Desperados that I remembered from the evening before which was already seeming like days ago.

Danny and I walked together to the cafeteria where a catered breakfast was waiting. As far as the eye could see and the stomach could imagine were mounds of eggs, pounds of bacon, and rivers of milk cartons. After filling a plate, I saw some of the other team members from Devo's Desperados sitting at a table and joined them. As I sat down, one of the other campers, Joe P, also called JP was already talking and filling everyone in on what to expect. The first thought I had was that there was already a JP on this team, and it was me; the second thing I thought was he is just one of those attention seekers and self-declared experts, but soon came to realize that he actually had a lot to contribute. Not only was he making sense in the things he said and clearly had some inside knowledge, but almost everyone in the room, former pros included, came up to address him in some form or fashion. I later found out that he had been attending this camp since Christ was a crossing guard! Not only that, but he also kept all the stats for all the players in the league for the entire week. My reservations were soon replaced with admiration, and I gave him my full attention.

Like everyone else had told us leading up to the camp, Joe P also emphasized that staying healthy was the key to enjoying the week. He told stories of how so many people came to play and after going too hard in the first game or two, they soon were sitting out due to a pulled hamstring or other host or injuries that could easily plague the over-forty generation. While I knew I wasn't in the playing shape of my youth, I still felt like I could hold my own. Soon after the rehashing of not overdoing it, our two coaches sat down. As part of Devo's Desperados, we had Ross Grimsley and Mike Devereaux as our coaches. They asked us what positions we played or wanted to play, and each of us provided an answer. Along with myself and Danny, there was the already-mentioned, Joe P, as well as Brad Dietz, Richard Claypool, Jeff Stratmeyer, Peter Sharp, Todd Hyson, Jeff Wolff (later voted MVP), Jack Byrd, and otherwise known as the Dynamic Duo, Amy Esterle, and Tricia Smith. That was our twelve-man team, sorry, our twelve-person team.

We sat around the table giving a little background of ourselves and why we were so passionate about the Orioles that we decided to do this Dream Week. About half of the team was returning players and half were rookies such as me. While I was envious of those who had the honor of playing in previous years and a better grasp on what to expect, it was also nice at the ripe old age of forty-nine to be a rookie. When asked by the coaches about what other positions I would like to play, I was a little bit taken back. All I had ever really done was pitch, minus my little league experience in right field. Yes, you know who plays right field in little league so that was not a great memory for me. I shrugged and said, being a left hander, I guess I could play a little first base. I hadn't realized at the time that I was setting up for more time at first base than being on the mound. The pitching was restricted by innings per game and day so there was a good chance that the majority of the players on the team would have an opportunity to pitch.

Just as we were getting into a rhythm of what positions we would like to play, they announced that there would be no games due to the condition of the field and that they would try to play a game in the afternoon for all teams. I was, to say the least, a bit disappointed, but our coaches took us to the outfield and had us field some ground balls and make some throws. Those who wanted to play outfield were taken to the other side of the left field line, and one of the coaches was hitting fly balls. I was doing just fine in the position of pitcher, covering the imaginary first base on any pitch hit to the right side, highlighting my expert knowledge of the position and the game.

Thinking back, I hadn't played outfield in any type of game since high school. The only time I did play outfield was during batting practice on my off days from pitching shagging fly balls and trying to get them on or in the bucket behind second base. Anyone who ever played the game knows exactly what I am talking about, those of you who haven't I will quickly explain. During batting practice there are screens and ball buckets set up throughout the outskirts of the infield where ground balls are being hit to the infielders while someone is also taking batting practice. The balls that make it into the outfield are corralled by anyone in the outfield area to include pitchers. Just behind second base they have a protective screen set up and someone manning a bucket. When anyone in the outfield gets a ball, they are to throw it into the person or area of the bucket to be collected and in intervals taken to the mound for the pitcher to continue using for batting practice. The game that we played was to try and throw the ball either in the bucket on one hop or as close to the bucket as possible.

On one occasion when I was shagging balls in the outfield, our catcher was hitting before the game and hit a fly ball to the outfield. I leisurely jogged back and reached up for it, but it went just over my head and over the shortest part of the home run fence which stood only about five feet high. The few people that were there early for the game and were actually paying attention to batting practice began to jeer at me, and I could even hear our catcher from the batter's box laughing his ass off at my lackluster performance. Despite all the times I had hit the bucket on my return throws, I suddenly lost all credibility. Shamefully and quietly, I took the mocking from the fans and returned to my position. After several line drives, our catcher, still at the plate, got into one, deep, deep, way back and I was on my horse this time. I turned and burned, running as hard as I could for the warning track. Looking over my shoulder, I could see the trajectory of the ball coming toward me, and just as I reached up to secure the catch, I crashed violently into the wall, almost propelling myself over the fence into the stands; but falling hard on my back, I felt myself gulp and the wad of chewing tobacco slide down my throat. As I writhed in pain, throwing up from the disgust and poisoning of the chewing tobacco, I was placed on a stretcher and carried off the field. X-rays at the hospital would reveal a cracked rib and broken sternum. After several weeks on the disabled list, I returned to my duties to include shagging fly balls, but from that day on, no pitcher was allowed to go past any area where the warning track met the field to shag balls during batting practice.

While I didn't use chaw anymore, there were still plenty of other embarrassing reasons to not want to play the outfield. As our morning session of infield/outfield drills concluded on the outfield grass, they let us know that we would have the opportunity to eat lunch and see the trainers before our opening game that afternoon. Instinctively, when we went back to the cafeteria, we got lunch and all sat down as a team. It was amazing how just a little bit of time together practicing and having fun, despite the many dropped and missed balls, made us a solid unit.

By noon, we were all looking at the board to see how the games would be divided. I was pleased to see that for the first game of the week, we were the visiting team which meant that I got to wear black, and with my mid-section curve, it was best that I wore black as often as possible. It is not that image is that important, but they would be taking photos that I would treasure for the rest of my life and wanted to be able to exaggerate the stories of my exploits without the exaggeration of my mid-section immediately bringing my stories into the fiction arena. So, with that I got on my uniform and posed for another picture by my locker and then headed out to our field. I walked down the concrete path to the dugout area, and it was just as I had imagined during my bus ride in. The same feeling of the plastic cleats, we weren't allowed metal for obvious reasons, the smells, sounds, all of it was a rush of familiarity and I was once again a ball player. Thrust back in time. One week of immortality was about to commence even if delayed for another day due to weather.

PLAY BALL!

It was Tuesday, the 29th of January. The rain finally subsided, and we had a clear yet chilly morning. I was now getting into the rhythm of the bus ride and structure of the area and felt much more comfortable in my routine even though it was just one extra day. After putting on my uniform and making my way to the correct field we were playing on, I was very excited when I got to the dugout to see our coach, former pro Ross Grimsley, filling out the starting lineup. Way down, batting at position nine, I saw my name and there was the number one beside it meaning that I was going to be the opening day starting pitcher. Suddenly, I felt a release of butterflies fill my stomach and my heart rate began to increase. Without exerting any effort, my palms began to sweat, and my mouth was becoming dry. I quickly recognized that my energy level was increasing and that I was losing my IZOF (Individual Zone of Optimal Functioning). IZOF was familiar to me as it was something I taught as an instructor with the soldiers in the Army. I also knew the best way to counter it was to take a few deep, deliberate breaths which I did. As if letting your foot off of the accelerator, my engine began to slow down, the heart rate lowered, saliva came back into my mouth and the butterflies began to dissipate. With my energy level now in check, I was ready to begin my throwing routine as I did before any start.

I told Danny, who would be catching me for that first start, that I would get loose and then be ready to throw in about fifteen minutes. I took the ball in the glove down the left field line by myself. I gently dropped the glove to the ground and began my stretching routine. Head and neck to shoulders, shoulders to arms, arms to the abdomen, and continued down the body. Once stretched and a productive sweat now going, I jogged from foul line to center field and back. Changing between high knees to over exaggerated strides. After a few of those and realizing I was now beginning to breathe a bit heavier, I summoned Danny down the line for me to begin my throwing routine.

Almost instinctively, I took my position about three paces in front of the bottom part of the mound where I played catch with Danny. From a short distance, I had him move the glove around to different target areas and would focus my throws to those areas. After several minutes, I then took my position about three paces from the farthest part of the back of the mound and began the same type of throwing routine. This time focusing on follow through and exaggerating my arm length to feel my release point. Once I was comfortable in that routine, I had Danny squat down behind the plate. The difference between the bullpen and the game, I let Danny know what pitch I was going to throw by flicking my glove hand forward for a fast ball, across and down the body for a curve, and a quick front to back motion for the change up. As I rotated through my pitches, keeping the magic twenty-five to thirty pitch count in my head, I felt my body return to a once glorified form.

WHEN THE FANS GO HOME

Completing my pre-performance routine, I walked slowly and deliberately back to the dugout. My jacket over my right arm, ball, and glove curled up over the jacket. I felt the transfer of my cleats from the grass of the outfield to the dirt of the one deck area and then to the concrete of the dugout. We all met at the front of the dugout, and as the coaches gave some preparatory speech, my mind was on the sequence of pitches and the anticipation of hearing the umpire point to me on the mound and yell those immortal words, "Play Ball." As the home team, we took the field first. As I ran out to the mound jumping over the foul line, I chuckled to myself that despite all my knowledge and training on performance optimization, I still couldn't shake some of the embedded superstitions I had surrounding the game.

We have all heard about superstitions either from people we've played sports with or through different movies. There is the classic one in *Bull Durham* where having sex might end the winning streak, or in the movie *Major League* where JoBu was given rum and cigars to take the curse off of the bats. I suppose for me the superstitions began around high school once I made the varsity team. Some of them have stayed with me all my life and became unconscious habits. For example, I always put on my left sock before my right, left pants leg, left shirt sleeve, etc. I did take notice in my forties that the one thing I did differently when my eyesight started getting worse is that I put my right contact in before my left. It almost felt weird to go out of order in my subtle but nearly obsessive-compulsive order of operations.

Superstitions in sports are usually minor, and for the most part quirky but harmless. The line gets crossed when a superstition is something that may be out of our control, and we insist our performance is related to it. I had a friend who I played summer ball with, and he insisted on getting a chili hot dog at the 7-Eleven before each game. I have had those chili hot dogs and can attest that there is no way they help with performance.

Anyway, running late to a game we stopped at the local 7-Eleven and they had no chili dogs ready. We did not have time to go to another store, and when we got to the field, he was so enraged and distraught he said he couldn't play the game. Imagine taking yourself out of a competition because you could not get a hot dog!

That is why I made sure any quirks or superstitions I had were almost always within my control, putting on my socks and shoes a certain way, hopping over the foul line to and from the dugout, and of course never shagging fly balls during batting practice. Well, that one was more of a mandate. My thoughts returned back to the present moment and took the ball off of the mound that the umpire had placed there. Just as in the bullpen prior to the game, I motioned for Danny to squat behind the plate, and I took my eight warmup pitches. On my last pitch, I pointed to the second baseman and shortstop and let them know the next one was coming down. Once I delivered the pitch, I exaggerated my follow through to the third base side as I didn't want to be anywhere in the vicinity of the throw from Danny to second base. As he hurled the baseball in the direction of second base, it came up short and one hopped the second baseman who tossed it to the shortstop who then threw it over to the third baseman who, in turn, was about to throw it to the first baseman before I put my hands up and yelled, "NO! It comes to me." Oh yeah, I forgot about that superstition.

Once I retrieved the ball from the third baseman ,who may have committed a horrible error of judgment by throwing it to the first baseman, I gathered myself and ceremoniously took the ball to the mound. From behind the pitching rubber, I bent down as I had done since college and picked up some of the dirt, rubbing it in between my hands then smelling it, bringing all my senses together. I stood fully upright, extending my arms to the side while taking a deliberate breath. As I walked to the top of the hill, I threw the ball firmly into my glove and zoned in on Danny setting up behind the plate.

I took the sign, fastball, and from the full windup rocked back, came to a balance point, and extended my arms out, feeling the stitches of the ball become one within in fingers, gripped loosely but securely. My momentum began to shift forward and like a snake ready to strike, I came from a coiled position and thrust myself forward toward the plate, striking at my opponent with venomous heat, or so it felt. The pitch sailed high and away from the right-handed hitter. I knew immediately that I was opening my right shoulder and not following through as well as having an early release point. I made adjustments throughout the inning but had a performance more resembling Ebby Calvin Laloosh than my idol Scott McGregor who had precise control and mastery of his curveball. After pitching three innings, I had four strikeouts, five walks, and two hits with only one run scored which, considering the circumstances of our defense, was more than acceptable. I didn't play a defensive position after my three innings so while the rest of the team was on the field, I was getting pitching advice from our coach and former big leaguer Ross Grimsley. The fact that he even took the time to help me was an acknowledgement that he accepted me as a pitcher, which was the most impressive part of the game. From that outing on, it was suggested that I pitch from the stretch position which made sense since it would limit the number of body parts I would have moving at the same time. Also, since I wasn't breaking any speed records there was no need for me to go from the full windup. The only disadvantage of pitching from the stretch was that there was no stealing, and even with my great move, I envisioned that attempting a pick-off move would result in a ball rolling into the opposing dugout or, even worse, up the right-field line.

Once the first game ended in victory and with an undefeated record thus far, it was time to grab a bite to eat and prepare for the second game of the day. We had been told that since we missed out on a day, the tradition of playing a visiting team from the Pittsburgh Pirates dream camp would not happen. Also, the coach's pitch game on Wednesday would be substituted for a double header so that each team got to play every other team that week. With that, we all made our way back to the locker room area. Once inside, I figured I might as well get an ice down and some massage from the trainers so I'd be ready to go the very next game. As I made my way to the training room, there was a line of about twelve people in front of me and six or more people already being treated. It was clear that after just one game, this was going to be a long week! Like an assembly line of broken parts being put together, we each made our way forward. I was given two bags of ice, one to be wrapped around my elbow and the next wrapped around my shoulder. With little attention given, I made my way back out to the locker room and allowed the ice to melt away on my arm before getting ready for the afternoon game.

After about twenty minutes, I took the half-melted bag of ice that was now dripping down my arm and dried it with a towel. The familiar tingling and numbness of many years of icing let me know that the healing process had begun. But unlike when I pitched years ago, I didn't have days to recover, only hours. I dried my arm off and took a couple of Tylenol to relieve any inflammation that may have occurred. With the pressure of the first start behind me, I felt more relaxed, and knowing I would come out of the bullpen gave me more time to control and manage my energy. The second game was in our favor for most of the early innings until a couple of errors cost us the lead. I came in relief and pitched much more effectively from the stretch position though we were never able to come back from the deficit of those early innings and errors. Despite going from the prospect of an undefeated season to .500 in just a few hours, we were all gelling and becoming closer as a team and all in all having a great time. Just like that, the first day was in the books.

As I was preparing to put my uniform in the laundry bin to be cleaned for the next day, I saw Patrick coming in from his game. He told me that his leg was hurting and more specifically that his quad was tight. I informed him of the line I had endured after the first game and encouraged him to see the trainers early as the mad rush was coming. Even as he limped in discomfort to the training room, he couldn't resist a Seinfeld reference by yelling, "Jimmy's Down." An episode where a character Jimmy always referred to himself in third person and had an injury in the locker room after Kramer spilled water on the floor. We continued to banter "Jimmy" lines back and forth and suddenly noticed people looking at us as we grew into a boisterous laughter. I decided to wait in line with him figuring that another ice pack wouldn't be a bad idea for me. As he made his way to the training table, I wished him well and went on my way.

After getting my second ice pack, I grabbed a couple of cold beers out of the huge tubs that were provided throughout the locker room for all the players. While I waited for Patrick to get his treatment done, I put my uniform on the string as instructed the day before so it would be washed and clean for the next set of double headers the following day. After a short while, Patrick came out and informed me that he took the ice bath and recommended I do the same. I reminded him of the "shrinkage" that would occur and that I was too much like George from Seinfeld and couldn't handle the criticism that would inevitably come from that event. With day one in the books, we made our way back to the hotel and agreed that after a shower we would meet in the downstairs lounge area.

As we were sharing stories and tall tales of our exploits in the first two games of the week and listening to the pros share more stories of their playing days, a quiet roar began to fill the area. As I looked around the corner, there he was, the legend of legends, the greatest third baseman to ever play the game, Brooks Robinson. He was seated with a few other people at a table just feet away as the crowd reluctantly gathered trying to get a glimpse of their idol while still respecting his privacy. Any anonymity was going to be futile on his part, and with much grace he waved and began allowing people to take photos with him. I made my way and really cannot recall anything that I said but just basked in the moment of being in the presence of such greatness.

It quickly came to memory that I had been in his presence once before. When I turned eighteen years old, my mother wrote to him telling him of the time when I was in kindergarten when we were told to write a letter, I wrote my very first letter to him. In return, he sent me an autographed picture and a copy of his book. Some twelve years later, once again he graced me with a letter in response to my mother. This time it was not an autographed picture but an invitation to go to lunch. That spring afternoon, we met and ate together, talking baseball. I didn't think to get a picture or an autograph because at the time we were two ballplayers sharing baseball experiences. This time, however, I could simply be a fan and didn't hesitate to get my picture taken with him. As time has passed and I have spoken with other campers who were present when Brooks made his appearance, all almost unanimously agree that seeing and meeting him was the highlight of the week.

As Wednesday approached and we made our way to the field, we found out that another former Oriole great pitcher, Jim Palmer, was going to be present along with Brooks. We also found out that they would both pose with each camper for a picture. As I prepared to pitch in my third game and was starting to feel some muscle pain from probably overthrowing a bit, I turned around and right behind me was Jim Palmer. As I was debating on which pain reliever to take, Jim said that I should take a few gel caps and rub the contents of the gel directly on the painful area. I wasn't sure if he was kidding or being serious so when I asked one of the trainers, he informed me that Jim had some very unique remedies for sore or achy muscles. So, with that, I decided to give it a try. I am not sure if it genuinely helped or it was the placebo effect, but for a short time, I did feel less sore. At least for now.

In the first game of the second day, Wednesday, I was in the lineup starting first base. We had some struggles at the position in the second game of our double header the day before, so they decided to try me out at the position. While I had never played a single day at first base in my entire playing career, I had watched it being played and during batting practice would listen to the infield coaches tell the first baseman how to position himself behind the bag and a few steps to the second base side of the infield. With that knowledge, I took the position, remembering to have a ball in my glove so that I could throw ground balls to the other position players while the pitcher warmed up before each inning. It was in throwing these ground balls that I realized my arm was much more fatigued than I had thought, and my quads were quite tight and sore. I had a fleeting thought that maybe I should have taken that ice bath.

As the game went on, my legs were becoming more and more stiff, and I realized that I was suffering from DOMS or Delayed Onset of Muscle Soreness. I walked my first at bat; the second time, I drove the ball deep in the gap and was able to turn a sure double into a long single. With each defensive inning, I became more and more comfortable at the position and even started having some fun conversations with anyone who got on first base. I would tell the base runner at first to go ahead and take a bigger lead and then run behind them to the bag as if a pick-off play was on, or I would kick dirt behind them to simulate my movement. At one point, the first base coach for the opposing team, former Pro Gregg Olson, was bantering back and forth with me to shut up and leave his players alone. Probably the most memorable thing that happened in that game though was when one half of the dynamic duo, Amy, was hit with a pitch directly on her backside. She didn't flinch nor did she heed the advice of teammate

Jeff Wolfe to rub it. I think we were all impressed with her even more after that.

After the first game, our team had little time to prepare as we ate a quick lunch and headed off to the second game at Ed Smith Stadium. This was the nicest field of all and was where the Orioles major league team played their spring training games. Between the two games, though, before we left there were grab bags of balls that could be purchased at fifty dollars apiece. Since the balls were in paper bags, it was random which ball you would get, but I purchased four of them. Two of the four were gold mines from previous seasons and one had Earl Weaver, Jim Palmer, Frank and Brooks Robinson, and a host of other players from the 1971 team. I didn't have much time to look at them, so I secured them in my locker and headed to the bus for the second game.

Playing at Ed Smith Stadium was certainly a thrill, and even though I didn't pitch in that game and went 0-2 at the plate, I did make some good defensive plays at first base to help us secure the win. There were some great photos taken that I still look at often. There is one picture in particular that I really like where it is me and teammate Peter Sharpe standing on the dugout steps with the backdrop of the dugout bench and wall behind us. Two ball players just sharing a simple moment. It was so typical of how that week would go, obscure moments that would become part of treasured memories. As we boarded the bus to go back to the locker room, we were informed that we were the last team to finish our games and that we would need to hurry and prepare for the evening ahead. In emails before camp and from day one, it was emphasized to not try and get autographs and such with the former pros because there would be a barbecue dinner where everyone would attend and there, we could get all the autographs we wanted.

I returned back to the hotel to quickly shower and get ready for the barbecue dinner. I met up with Patrick at the entrance and we both went together with a group to the gift shop where we could purchase items as souvenirs or to be signed by the players at the conclusion of the dinner. Patrick made it known that he was not much of an autograph collector, which was very different from my approach. I came out of the gift shop with helmets, hats, balls, even a shirt and pair of shorts. I don't recall how much I spent, but I had two full bags. When we returned to the dining area, we ate and then got in line to meet the players who were sitting two at a table ready to sign autographs. Even with all I had bought, I still needed to purchase a few pictures of the individual players to have them signed, as well. Toward the end of the evening, I even got another picture with my hero, Scott McGregor, whose team we would be facing in game two of the following day. After an exhausting full day, we headed back to the hotel where my roommate was already asleep. It occurs to me that he seemed to always be asleep whenever I came into the room in the evening or left in the morning. He never hung out with me or anyone else that I know of. I assume he played the games but can't even recall what team he was on.

That was one of the things that made Dream Week so fascinating. Not only the former pros but also the other campers. So many people from all walks of life. Everything from a state senator to a helicopter pilot, from doctors to delivery drivers. People who lived from California to Pennsylvania and everywhere in between, all coming together for the common love of baseball and the Orioles. Playing double headers every day and dinners or banquets almost every night ,it was hard to get to know everyone at the camp while it was happening. Even getting to know everyone on your team could be challenging, but there were always moments that made the connection possible.

In the mornings during breakfast in the cafeteria they would hand out gold and brown ropes to players on each team who did something exceptional, gold rope, or who made a memorable blunder, brown rope. I remember that I received a gold rope early in the week for a pitching performance, but more importantly, I was happy that I didn't get a brown rope. One of the best brown ropes given out that I can remember was given to the pitcher of the opposing team who beamed Amy, one of the dynamic duo from our team. What made it even better was that Amy was in no way shy of lowering her pants to show everyone the bruise she received from that. Those were just some of the moments that brought everyone together.

Another great thing about the breakfast time in the cafeteria was the stories that pros would tell. I am not going to give them away here in this book. If you want to hear them, you'll just have to sign up to go to a Dream Week of your own. What I will say is that no matter how many times they have probably been asked to share their favorite moments, each of them was gracious enough to share them with us again as if it was the first time they were ever told. I will share that one of the highlights was the story Brooks told about going to make a guest appearance at a retirement community. Brooks said that when he entered, he asked one of the young attendants at the front desk if the attendant knew who he was and where he should go and the attendant replied, "No sir, but if you just head down the hallway, I'm sure one of the staff members can tell you who you are and where your room is." That was just the kind of week it was, lots of laughs and authenticity.

It is funny to me that as I recall the events and days of Dream Week, it seemed like such a long time that we spent together. It is remarkable to me as I write this is that all the games occurred in just four days. So many vacations and events that I have attended in the past seemed to fly by and were just a blur, but Dream Week was so rich and full and so much happened in such a short time it seems like I was there for several weeks. I guess that is also part of the magic of Dream Week and why I would advocate for anyone considering it to go. I have had a lot of great experiences, traveled to amazing destinations, met some famous people, but none of those other experiences are so sustainable over time and while they may have been worth writing home about, they certainly weren't worth writing a book about. Somehow though, this experience brought all my education, knowledge, history of the game, and love of the Orioles together.

By Thursday, we were halfway through playing and were a salty 2-2 but gaining momentum. While I pitched two innings and played first base, got a couple more hits and we won game one on the day, it was really the second game I was looking forward to. It was my opportunity to have my childhood hero, Scott McGregor, watch me pitch. In between the two games, I got ice and my bicep muscle was beginning to get worn, but there was no way I was going to be less than perfect for this performance. I rested the first couple of innings not playing the field before taking the hill with the ball. As I stood on the mound, I recalled watching the mechanics of Scott McGregor for months leading up to Dream Week and thought back to my home-made pitching mound in Bristol Tennessee where I started imitating his delivery. A full extension of both arms from the midsection out and up like a bird taking flight and then to the swooping three quarter delivery whipping my arm down and across my body. It was an orchestra of imitation, and I felt like a king on that hill.

I came up to bat in the second to last inning and hit a ball sharply to right field. As I took my lead from first base, a hard ground ball was hit by teammate Jack Byrd. While I knew Jack was not the most fleet of foot as most of us at our age are no longer the speed demons we once were, I thought the only chance he had was for me to break up the double play. So instinctively I went into second base, a perfect hook slide and put the opposing second baseman in the dirt. Jack made it to first, and I was able to walk off the field with dignity knowing that I broke up the double play cleanly, and most importantly, no one got hurt or pulled any muscles in the process.

I barely had time to catch my breath and get a quick drink of water before taking the field again to pitch the final inning in a tight game. Even in the warmup pitches, I could tell that I was getting a dead arm. A heaviness and ache in my bicep and two-time surgically repaired shoulder. I stood on the mound and took a few deliberate breaths telling myself that all the training I had done, every mile I had run, every long toss I threw to a backstop was all for this moment. I walked the first hitter of the inning, a cardinal sin when pitching with a lead in the late innings. The next hitter popped the ball up over the mound behind me. Not high enough for any infielder to get to it, so I turned my back to the plate and made an incredible over the shoulder basket catch, quickly turning toward first base to try and double up the runner, but unfortunately, the opposing baserunner had more faith than I did that I could catch the ball. In hindsight, if I had let the ball drop, I probably could have turned a double play with no infield fly rule in effect. Of course, then again, that may have risked an errant throw and could have had first and third with no one out.

The next batter hit a fly ball that was caught by the sure-handed Jeff Statamyer, and I was one courageous out away from securing the win. I really wanted to record a strikeout to finish the game in honor of Scott McGregor, though ironically it would be his team I would be beating. Each pitch I would feel the tingling and numbness followed by sharp pain in my arm, and with a couple foul balls and pitches on the outside I found myself in a full count against the hitter. I thought to myself that I had one great curveball left in me and what better way to finish the game than on a curveball while the master curveball pitcher looked on. I reared back, making sure my elbow was above my shoulder as I started to rotate forward, telling myself "snap it off." I released the pitch and knew as soon as I let it go that it was going to fall off the table, down and in on the hands of the right-handed hitter. Sure enough, he was probably looking fast-ball on the full count, swung right over the top of it, and that was the game! After the initial high fives with each other and me securing the game ball, we met the opposing team at home plate and shook hands. There at the end of the line was their coach, Scott McGregor who shook my hand and commented on my good game.

Once again, I made my way to the locker room and right to the trainers as my arm was throbbing in pain. I let them know that my bicep was really hurting me, and I could hardly lift my arm up over my head. This time the trainers paid more attention to me than in previous days because I was in obvious pain. In three days, I had only pitched nine innings in the four games played, but due to my lack of control, I am sure my pitch count was pretty high. At least much more so than I had anticipated or trained for in the months prior to Dream Week. With another dose of anti-inflammatory medication, a quick massage, and another full-on ice pack, I made my way to the beer tubs and traditionally grabbed my two beers.

I met up with Patrick in the locker room who was telling me about his pitching performance. With his quad still hurting, he was doing more pitching than he expected because his range of motion was preventing him from playing his natural position at shortstop. As we loaded up on the bus to head back to the hotel, Patrick and I were sitting next to each other, and the row in front of us on the opposite side of the aisle was my brother-in-law, Danny. Danny had set his open beer on the floor and as the bus began to drift forward, it jerked a bit as buses often do and the beer Danny had on the floor toppled over and the contents began running down the entire length of the bus, flowing over and around unsuspecting people's bags beneath their seats. Instead of quickly grabbing the can, Danny looked aggravated as he muttered out, stupid ass bus driver. I looked at Patrick and gave him the inexplicable voice of the Tasmanian Devil, "oohblooahga" and we immediately burst into hysterical laughter as we often did. Patrick would later recall to me that sometimes when he was up to bat and was feeling a bit nervous, he would hear me in his mind making that noise and it would instantly relax him and make him laugh. I don't think that Danny shared in our appreciation for his likeness to the character, but it really was all in good fun.

The conversation turned to the final day of games as we rode back to the hotel. The final victory Devo's Desperados had in the afternoon game secured us a playoff spot as the number four seed. Patrick was sure that their team was the number one seed meaning that our first game the next day would be against Patrick's Team. We had faced them on Wednesday and lost so I was looking forward to once again getting a chance to play against him. I wasn't sure if I was going to pitch in that game since I had pitched several innings the day before. Patrick said that he did expect to pitch in the game so at least we would have that battle though all things being equal I would rather be on the mound. As we departed the bus, I had to quickly go upstairs and change for the team dinner that evening.

It is tradition at Dream Week that the players all go out to dinner with the coaches and that the players contribute to the coach's meal and a small gift. I have to be honest that I was not really keen on the idea considering what we had to pay for the week as a whole, but I was looking forward to eating in a nice restaurant and having a chance to learn more about the teammates I had begun to draw an authentic liking and connection to. Earlier in the week, I had snuck my vehicle back to the parking area of the hotel, so I was able to drive myself to dinner being that I was in the training room so long and late getting back. By the time I arrived, almost everyone was already there and seated. I got to sit next directly across from one of the nicest guys in the world, Richard. His wife was also in attendance, and I came to find out that not only was he a sure-handed second baseman who bailed me out of a covering first base on a grounder to the right side, but he was a curator at Gettysburg, Pennsylvania. Directly next to Richard was our coach, Ross Grimsley, and his wife. They shared the story about how they met and how Ross had to pursue her relentlessly. What struck me the most here was a pitcher that had been in some tremendous pressure situations pitching at the highest level, and yet their ability to be so raw and authentic was remarkable. In those moments and in reflection since, the most common theme that comes to mind is that I was just surrounded by not only elite athletes of their time, but very good human beings. That goes for the players I had the honor of sharing the ballfield with as well.

After dinner I returned to my room, entering quietly as my roommate, of course, was already asleep. I was trying to recall the previous day's games to remember our overall record and who we beat or lost to, but all the previous days were running together. I could not believe that one, we only had one day left and two that we had a chance to win the overall championship. I will confess that while part of me was a little sad that it was coming to an end, another part of me was extremely relieved because my quads and pitching arm were tight and ragged out, respectively. Winning the championship was not just ceremonial in nature. The winning team got a pretty nice championship ring, too. Danny was on the winning team two years prior and never gave up the opportunity to show his ring off. Not only did each player get a ring, depending on what they wanted to spend, it got presented to them on the field at Camden Yards during a pre-game ceremony to an Orioles regular season game, which would also be really cool. With thoughts of a championship in my mind, I faded off to sleep.

THE CHAMPIONSHIP ROUND

The next morning, I woke up and prepared for our championship game. My roommate was on one of the teams that was not in the championship round and so they played a runner-up type tournament with two games to round out fourth through eighth place. For the final time, I put on my cutoff Oriole's t-shirt with shorts, my Orioles beanie hat and took my place on the bus. Just as I had done every other morning, I put my earbuds in and listened to music on the way in, spending some time visualizing the upcoming game and how I wanted to perform. Having a routine for even just a few days made me feel much more ready and comfortable. I made my way to my locker and, as expected, saw the schedule of games. We were playing against Patrick in the morning game as the one and four seed while the two and three seed played, and the winner of each of those games would play for the ring and title of 2019 Dream Week Champions. Sitting at breakfast and listening to the stories being told of the week and other antics of the former pros, I felt something I hadn't felt in a long time. I felt butterflies in my stomach, and it dawned on me, this game really mattered, and I wanted to perform well. After breakfast, I made my way back to the locker room from the cafeteria and put on my full uniform, and made the slow, deliberate walk down the sidewalk to the field. I checked the lineup card and saw that I was going to be starting at first base. Both coaches came over to me and let me know that they wanted to save me for the championship game if we got there, but either way, I would be pitching in game two of the day.

As the visiting team, we had first at bat. Though I didn't get a plate appearance, we took a quick lead due to some walks and timely base hits. After the top half of the inning, we were up one to nothing. The first inning defensively was uneventful with only one runner getting on base. Ironically, it happened to be the pitch runner for Patrick who was still ailing his injured leg. The top of the second inning we got a few more walks and scored another run. Defensively in the bottom of the second inning I almost made a diving play to stop a ball on the right side of the infield, and by saying I almost made a diving play what I mean is that about the time the ball hit the outfield grass my momentum carried me to the ground. I did end up with a very nice raspberry on my right arm that still has remnants of scar. When I got to my feet, I looked at the opposing first base coach who happened to be Gregg Olson and asked him if I was close to knocking that ball down. Without hesitation and with strong conviction he said, "No, not close." The opposing team scored two runs in their half of the inning and tied the game at two apiece.

    I was in the on-deck circle for the third inning when the opposing team made a pitching change, Patrick was in the game. I was going to get to face Patrick for the first time. I remember thinking as I walked up to the plate to just focus on the release point and get the bat through the zone. All my concentration went out the window when I looked out at Patrick, and he was looking back at me with an unconcerned cheesy grin on his face. I was in peril, and he was having the time of his life. I took two deliberate breaths and stepped in. Rocking my bat back and forth like the pendulum on a grandfather clock getting my rhythm waiting for him to go into his delivery. Just as he was about to release the ball, I heard him laugh and the pitch came right down the middle and suddenly dropped out across the plate for a ball one call. It was the best movement on a ball I had seen all week, and suddenly, I realized that he had undersold his ability to pitch. I moved up in the box knowing that if he threw the same pitch, I would want to get it before the break. Again, he delivered, and before the ball had a chance to leave my imaginary hitting box, I got the best part of the bat on the ball. I completely tattooed the ball into deep left field. It was by far the best contact I had made all week. I sprinted as best I could at first, looking up and seeing the left fielder extend his glove into the blue sky and robbing me of the best hit I would have had all week. Patrick would later confess to me that he didn't think the left fielder was going to make the catch based on previous attempts earlier in the week. That bit of information only made it sting a little more.

    The game continued and Patrick's team got the upper hand, taking a five to two lead. It was the last at bat for our resilient Devo's Desperados and we were indeed getting desperate because Patrick had shut us down. He was still pitching in the last inning, and I considered being in the five spot I might have a slim chance to face him again. As fate would have it, that is exactly what happened. We had two outs and two men on. While I was the tying run, it was not in my thought at the time of the possibility I could provide the Earl Weaver special (a three-run homer for you non-Orioles fans). My goal was just to extend the inning and keep bringing people to the plate. I had told other hitters to watch that natural tail that Patrick had on his ball, and now it was time to heed my own advice. I stepped up to the plate again, taking my purposeful pendulum timing batting approach I had seen from great hitters like Cal Ripken and Ichiro Suzuki. The first pitch was delivered and was right down the middle. I took a hack but fouled it off- straight back. I had a mental recollection that if a hitter fouls a pitch straight back then they are on it. Suddenly I had the voice of Crash Davis in my head saying, "Throw that shit again meat". The next two pitches were balls, and I was up in the count, two balls and one strike. I knew I could be more selective and so as I had taught so many players before me, I drew that imaginary little box in front of home plate where I wanted the ball to be. If the ball wasn't in that box, I would let it go. It didn't concern me to take another strike, after all I hadn't struck out all week. As he delivered the pitch, I saw it start to fall off and I let it go, but the umpire seemed to think that it got the outer edge of the plate and called it a ball. Now even in the count, I knew he would come back with the same pitch. I told myself, "Just go with it to right field." Just as I anticipated, the pitch started over the middle of the plate and began falling off, but this time with more conviction. My momentum, already going forward, I stayed back on the ball, turned for the inside out swing, but to my surprise, the ball escaped the bat. Strike three was called and the game was over.

My instinct was to toss my bat down in disgust, and I have to give full disclosure, my first thought was both a few expletives along with a physically impossible task to do to myself. What happened after that was remarkable though and was the springboard for me even thinking about writing this book. I realized in the midst of my despair as I looked out at the pitching mound and saw Patrick celebrating with his team another emotion, one totally unexpected and foreign in any other competition that mattered in which I lost. The emotion was gratitude. I was grateful not for losing, but that I got to see my friend celebrate in victory. It did not lessen the desire I had to win or the suck of making the last out, but it did give me an authentic experience in which appreciation was the overriding feeling I had. It was in that moment standing on the side watching the celebration that I finally got everything I had gone to grad school and been taught. The true meaning of competition and the end result of really performing at your best.

The fact that Patrick gave his best and that I gave my best was the reward, not the outcome. Knowing that just a few innings before I had drilled a pitch off him that was caught miraculously by their left fielder that could have turned the tide in our favor helped me understand in that moment that it's not about the outcome, it's about the effort, the experience, and the awareness that sometimes you come out on top and sometimes you come out on bottom, but showing up and doing your best is where the control lies. I think we all experience those "ah-ha" moments in our lives, but the key is learning from those moments and harvesting that experience to make us the best we can be in any given situation. Of all the thrills and expectations that were exceeded during Dream Week, nothing was greater than the experience of seeing and feeling competition at its finest.

Our team played in the consolation game against the loser of the other championship bracket, and we were winning until the last inning where I came in to pitch and ended up with my first and only loss of Dream Week. While the day had not gone anything as planned or what I visualized it would be on the bus ride to the facility that morning, it was something special. After our game, I went in and got ice as usual and took my anti-inflammatory medicine as usual and then made my way down to the main field where the final championship game was still going on. Along with many of the fellow campers, family, and pros, there was Scott McGregor sitting in a golf cart watching the game. I took my cleats that I custom ordered just for Dream Week and cleaned them the best I could, and Scott was gracious enough to autograph them both. They continue to sit proudly as the center mantlepiece about the fireplace. As the final inning began, I asked the score, and Patrick's team was winning, and Patrick was on the mound to close the game out. I sat back and watched, feeling excited for every pitch he threw until the very last one where a ground ball out secured the victory and championship for his team. The celebration was emotional for me to watch, not because I was upset it wasn't our team, but because I knew they had to get past our team to win it all. I was proud of Patrick and everyone on his team. The celebration was genuine and enthusiastic. It was evident that it meant something to all of them to win which made losing to them a little easier to acknowledge. It was amazing to me that less than a week ago, I first met this squirrelly guy in the lobby of the resort, neither of us knowing anything or anyone and now sharing in this moment knowing that I had developed a true, lasting friendship with him. Of all the things I expected, I never expected to develop such kinship with so many people in such a short amount of time, and now it was just about over.

    With the final game played, I made my way back up to the facility and changed for the last time out of my Orioles uniform. I packed up my bags and gifts that had accumulated in my locker over the week and made my way to the bus. With my last two beers in hand, I made my way to the bus and tried to recall the day and week that had preceded both so quickly and also seemed to last forever. I made my way to the hotel and had my last photo op with my Scott McGregor signed cleats. As I went into the room and started packing things into my bags, I could not believe how many souvenirs, autographs, and items I had bought in the few days there. I was also thankful that I had driven and not flown because there is no way I would be able to pack all this in just a few bags. The entire back of my SUV would be full of keepsakes, pictures, and additional gear. I also had packed two week's worth of business casual clothes since I was going directly from Sarasota to Fort Rucker, Alabama, for training. The only remaining time we would have together was at the upcoming banquet. With that, I took my shower and met Patrick in the lobby of the resort. We had a pre celebratory final drink and made our way up to the banquet room.

THE BANQUET AND GOODBYES

Upon entering the banquet room, I found tables set up for each team. As I gazed around, I took inventory of what I observed and quickly realized that the people who were strangers to me just six days ago would become lifelong friends. I joined my team, and we shared stories and elaborations of the great feats and performances we had experienced. Upon reflection, with the exception of my closest battle buddies with whom I served in the military, I've never felt closer to a group of individuals. And just as it is with any group of comrades, friends, or teammates, some inclusive hazing and practical jokes were to be expected. This band of brothers, and dare I say sisters, were never void of such opportunities; and on this night, I was their target.

I made my way around to the other tables, stopping and chatting with other Dream Week participants. The mistake I made was leaving my phone unattended at the team table. I didn't notice until a few days later, but my fellow teammates had taken fifty pictures or more with my cell phone. Although I opted not to share the photos in this book, I still find it hard to believe that some of the most prominent people in baseball, business, law, education, and aviation would conduct themselves in such a manner. Of course, I say that in jest because even as I write this chapter, I find myself looking, reflecting, and laughing at the pictures I still have on my phone.

As the night progressed, it was difficult to believe that the week was coming to an end. At the same time, it was equally difficult to believe that it had only been a week. Sitting at the table and looking around as if in a bubble all my own, I could hear the announcements of awards being given out to those who played exceptionally well but only in the background of my consciousness as I was fully engaged in observing each of the players, coaches, and other participants. I wanted these images to be vivid in my memory so as never to forget this moment, as if I ever could. Since then, those "snapshots" and countless memories frequently cross my mind and bring an unexplained smile to my face.

As grand as the opening banquet began, this final banquet came to an end without fanfare. The filled room began to slowly empty as teammates and participants made it back to their rooms for final packing and preparations to return to their normal lives. I had an advantage in that I had driven and could travel at my convenience to my next location, one that would have me in vigorous classroom training for two weeks. The few of us who remained until late in the evening began sharing stories as if we had been playing together for years. We reminisced with the pros who shared some bits of history we hadn't known. It was remarkable to me in those moments how players I once felt were so unapproachable became naturally immortal. Still heroes of my childhood but now every bit as human with dreams, challenges, and life experiences as myself.

The next morning most of the participants had left before I even got out of bed, including my roommate who I never much associated with in either conversation or activity. I finished packing my bags, and with all the souvenirs I had amassed, I was very grateful not to have to figure out how to load everything into a checked bag. There was a farewell breakfast that I missed but was able to grab leftovers at the hotel. As I scraped the last bit of eggs from the metal catering pan and placed them onto a slice of bread for a makeshift sandwich, one of the pros who lives in the area came strolling in. Wearing a t-shirt with the sleeves torn off, blue Tommy Bahama beach shorts, and flip flops, his hair unkempt, he too was looking to scavenge the last bit of breakfast. We exchanged pleasant nods, and as I stood trying my best not to let the last bit of egg sneak out the bottom of my sandwich, he quietly asked with a raspy voice, "So did you have a good time?" I responded simply, "Time of my life." He again nodded in recognition, and I quietly left him to his private search and made my way back to my room.

Carrying my bags down to the car required several trips. On my last one, with nothing more than an over-the-shoulder duffle bag, I stepped out onto the balcony to enjoy the view of the white sand beaches and the serenity of the ocean breeze as I listened to the waves crash on the shoreline. I thought to myself what a great place this would be to relax. It dawned on me that with all that had been going on, before this moment I had never even acknowledged the beach view or the peaceful tranquility it provided. With one final snicker of ironic laughter, I thought to myself, *I'll be back one day* and headed for Alabama.

It was on that four-hour drive that I first conceptualized what a great book this adventure would be. That vision, some three years later, brought this story to you.

PART THREE
TAKING ACTION

GOAL SETTING

Explanation of the Goal Setting Sheet:
When determining a goal the first and most obvious question to address is What is my goal? After determining the goal it is important to understand the "why". The "why" is what will drive you to keep pushing forward when either your thoughts or your body wants you to quit and give up. The phrase, "conditions don't matter" is a reference to our "why". When considering the "why" it should include at least one value that the person possesses. For example, if I were to say I want a good job so I can support my family, that is too ambiguous and does not provide a value that someone has. If I were to say that my family has always been there for me no matter what and I want to achieve this goal so that I can be that support for them in times of need. It could also be that I want to make my family, partner, or self proud because being proud of what I do is important to me, it will be my legacy. Those last two statements indicate a value, something firm and solid that will not easily be persuaded against when obstacles present themselves. After determining the "why" and pulling on our value system to make our goal solidified, it is important to address the obstacles that may present themselves and to do this we make a list of benefits and obstacles

that will present themselves in the process of reaching our goal. When making this list, it is imperative to use mental contrasting meaning that one benefit, one obstacle, one benefit, one obstacle. This technique allows balance in understanding the rewards and challenges of reaching the goal. Once the list is complete take from the obstacles list and from that develop an action plan. The action plan is simply completing small goals that coincide with the primary goal. For example, if my goal was to run a marathon in under three hours, then my action plan may be to run five miles a day four days a week. To address the obstacles a priority area next to the action plan should be made. For example, if I am going to run five miles a day four days a week but it rains all week that could be an obstacle so my priority area will be, 'when it rains I will run on a treadmill at Planet Fitness'. For each obstacle there needs to be an action plan and priority area. Once all the planning is done, it is imperative to take immediate action. Pick one thing from the action plan that can be implemented in the next twenty four hours. As this is a fluid document and involved process, I recommend contacting me for additional consultation on how to best effectively develop and administer a goal plan.

STEP 1: DEFINING MY GOAL:

What is my Goal?

```
[                                                    ]
```

What is my why?

```
[                                                    ]
```

How will I measure my goal?

```
[                                                    ]
```

STEP 2: BEING REALISTIC

Mental Contrasting:

Benefits	Obstacles

STEP 3: BECOMING AWARE

Primary areas of Attention:

Needs To Be Addressed	SMART Ways to Meet Needs

STEP 4: BEGIN ACTION

Target Start Date: _____
1st Review Date: _____
Target End Date: _____

Building a routine:

Action to be taken	Routine to be used

Power Statements:

STEP 5: CONTINGENCY PLANNING

When/Then:

When this happens	I will do this

STEP 6: STAYING MOTIVATED

How will I set up my environment?

Who will I have as a support?

What will I do to sustain my motivation?

STEP 7: REVIEW AND ADAPT

Review Date:_____

Sustains	Improves	Adjust Areas of Attention

Mentoring/Coaching for Successful Performance:

The model of T.I.P.P.S. (Tell, Instruct, Practice, Perform, Support) was designed by myself and is based off of the Self-Determination Theory. Oftentimes employers may offer competitive pay and an adequate benefit package, but still have high turnover. High turnover and costs of training are some of the biggest impacts on production and profitability. If employees have a sense of belonging, value, autonomy, and purpose then while the pay is a contributing factor it is not the main factor as to why employees stay with a company or business. The T.I.P.P.S. model breaks down the process for training and support that covers the four basic areas that will allow businesses and teams to perform at their optimal level and do so consistently. For more information on how to implement this model in your business or team please reach out to me through my website https://www.quinnittowinit.com or email at winwithquinn22@gmail.com.

Tell- Why am I being instructed to do this?

Instruct- How do I do this?

Practice- When will I get to work on this?

Perform - When will I be evaluated on this?

Support - How will I continue to get better at this?

LEARN HOW TO DEAL WITH LOSING

The idea behind this worksheet is to understand how someone perceives losing versus how they feel like they should perceive losing. The first question is designed to relate feelings to losing. The words selected help an individual come to terms with the emotions they associate with losing. If the emotions are primarily punitive this could indicate a less effective thought process around losing. Once the "key words" are selected in regards to emotion, the worksheet then focuses on the thoughts and behaviors that occurred soon after a loss is experienced. To get the best benefit from this worksheet please contact me for additional consultation.

How did I feel after the loss?*(circle all that apply)

Angry	Grateful	Tired	Hopeful
Confident	Distrustful	Determined	Surprised
Hopeless	Apathetic	Strong	Focused
Satisfied	Hungry	Exhausted	Irritated
Cheated	Calm	Sick	Honored
Happy	Distant	Resolved	Desperate
Relieved	Purposeful	Appreciative	Driven

What did I think after the loss?

_____
_____
_____
_____
_____
_____
_____
_____

Who did I tell after the loss?

_____
_____
_____
_____
_____
_____
_____
_____

WHEN THE FANS GO HOME

What was my plan after the loss?

_____
_____
_____
_____
_____
_____
_____
_____
_____

What did I do after the loss?

_____
_____
_____
_____
_____
_____
_____
_____
_____

Fill in your own words:

_____
_____
_____
_____
_____
_____
_____
_____
_____

EPILOGUE

Since Dream Week and the inception of the idea of this book, there have been many life events, both personal and professional, that have shaped the direction I wanted to take with this book. Often in my professional life, I am referred to as a "motivational speaker," but motivational speakers typically give the same talk or lecture at every event, a one-size-fits-all approach. I hope the readers of this book can take from my experiences and apply the skills I have mentioned into their own lives. While I typically work with some of the most elite professionals in their field, it doesn't take an elite athlete to apply these skills, only an elite mindset. Competition should not be about beating your opponent; it should be about performing at your best and doing it consistently.

I continue to grow in both my work and life using the skills I address in this book: confidence, mindset, energy management, attention control, imagery, and resilience. This book is certainly not all-inclusive, and I encourage any reader to reach out to me and let me know not only your thoughts but also what else I can provide for your personal growth. I continue with consulting work and since this book, I have worked with soldiers, pilots, business executives, and athletes at all levels. The title of this book suggests that we don't need fans or large crowds to perform at our optimal level and compete to the best of our abilities. I hope in all performances you find the desire to be the best you can be and that his book will guide you in those attempts. Never be afraid to go outside your comfort zone, and remember that while we need success to build confidence, we sometimes need to fail in order to grow.

ACKNOWLEDGMENTS

There are many people to whom I owe a great deal of gratitude for making this book a reality. First and foremost, I have to thank my mother who, though not with us, was the inspiration for me to become a writer at an early age. I want to thank my father, who taught me that taking a risk is, if nothing else, a learning experience and that life should be lived in good conscience and integrity. He always insisted that my actions and words could either inspire or discourage me and always guided me toward inspiration.

I would be remiss if I failed to acknowledge the pros at Dream Week who allowed us to be both fans and teammates. I would especially like to thank my Dream Week managers, Mike Deveraux and Ross Grimsley, for their energy and genuine love of the game. To Mike Bordick and Gregg Olson who never shied away from sharing stories or providing feedback on our performance. To Scott McGregor who graciously spent time with me and accepted my fanatical fan-like memories with him. Finally, Steve Freeman and Bill Stetka who organized the Dream Week and made it all come together without a hitch.

To my teammates and fellow campers, especially Joe Pavlock, a seasoned vet who continues to be the glue that keeps everyone in contact. To Todd Hyson and the Wolfe who provided us with memorabilia at our reunion game. I still have the bat and the t-shirt.

To my brother-in-law, Danny, who without his past Dream Week experience and bravado over it, I never would have envisioned that I would have such an extraordinary adventure. I'm glad that we were able to share it and will be able to reminisce about it for years to come.

And Patrick Barrows, one of the best friends I could ever ask for. Though on another team, he made this incredible experience that much better.

There is one person not directly related to Dream Week but who was vital in this book's completion who deserves a great deal of recognition—Dave Williams—coworker and friend. At a time when I was struggling for the next chapter, and my word count was barely enough for a graduate paper, he encouraged me to just write in a way only he can persuade. Thank you, Dave, for always being there even when you didn't know you were.

Thank you, everyone.

ABOUT THE AUTHOR

J.P. received his Bachelor's Degree from Salisbury University Majoring in Psychology with a concentration in Industrial/Organization Psychology. He was a collegiate athlete and served as team captain of his College Baseball Team. After college, JP served in the Army with the 290th MP Co being honorably discharged in 2003. JP received the Meritorious Service Medal and Army Achievement Medal after responding with his Unit to the Pentagon following the terrorist attacks on 9/11. JP attended The University of the Rockies where he received his Master's Degree in Sport & Performance Psychology achieving a 4.00 GPA and induction to the Golden Key Honor Society.

J.P. started a **Baseball Academy** in 2014 focusing on the performance psychology of athletes, and was recruited in 2018 to work as a Master Resiliency Trainer and Performance Expert with Army Basic Combat Training Units at Fort Jackson as well as the Drill Sergeant Academy. In 2021, J.P. went on to work with the Air Force helping train fighter pilots at Columbus Air Force Base before taking up an academic position in Florida where he now calls home.

www.ingramcontent.com/pod-product-compliance
Lightning Source LLC
Chambersburg PA
CBHW060615080526
44585CB00013B/844